# HENRI SAMUEL

# HENRI SAMUEL
## MASTER OF THE FRENCH INTERIOR

EMILY EVANS EERDMANS

Forewords by JACQUES GRANGE
and EVA SAMUEL

*RIZZOLI*
NEW YORK

New York · Paris · London · Milan

# CONTENTS

# FOREWORD

*By Jacques Grange*

**IN 1965, THE YEAR OF MY TWENTY-FIRST BIRTHDAY,** I started a three-year internship with the decorator Henri Samuel, following my years at the École Boulle and the École Camondo in Paris. Being trained by this distinguished teacher was the best thing that ever happened to me.

My first job was the supervision of work done for the Grand Trianon at Versailles, which included historical research and the selection of textiles. André Malraux, minister of cultural affairs, had initiated the project to create a space to receive foreign guests of the Republic.

Thanks to Henri Samuel, I discovered the great classical tradition, the essence of quality, and the importance of collaboration with artists. Samuel was an undisputed master in his profession.

He created the most beautiful interiors for the Rothschild family: the Château de Ferrières for Baron and Baroness Guy de Rothschild, as well as the mansion in the Rue de l'Elysée and the reopening of the Château d'Armainvilliers near Paris for Baron and Baroness Edmond de Rothschild. All these residences were full of masterpieces and treasures.

As part of my duties, I oversaw the master's commissions by Diego Giacometti: a stair balustrade, low tables, among other designs. Diego was a very gentle and charming man, quietly working in his atelier in the rue Hippolyte-Maindron.

Henri Samuel approached other young and energetic sculptors and painters, such as Philippe Hiquily and Guy de Rougemont, and convinced them to create furniture for his installations.

I will never forget the day that Balthus arrived to hang a magnificent picture over Samuel's fireplace mantel.

The training I received at Henri Samuel served, and continues to serve, as a guide for all my work.

I am eternally grateful to him.

# FOREWORD

*By Eva Samuel*

**TO WRITE A FEW WORDS** to introduce this book on the life and work of my uncle Henri is a pleasure I am happy to take. Knowing little of his professional or even social life, it is through the eyes of a little girl that I recount the memories of my childhood, thanks to which I have built a world of reference where art, space, and well-being are omnipresent. It was not through verbal communication that my relationship with Henri was built, as children were not addressed in those times, but through the infusion of sensations I experienced in the places he lived. It is only later, through my reflections as an adult and continued visits to his homes, that I can interpret my uncle's great artistic vision.

**Decoration is much more than an art destined to be seen.**

The taste of wild strawberries served in a thin crystal bowl, fresh and peppery nasturtium from the garden thrown into a salad, the musky taste of the tarragon in buttery green beans, the tender veal Orloff served by the maitre d'hotel in white gloves.... These are the memories that reflect this atmosphere of the sensations and flavors framed in the refined elegance of his country house in Montfort.

In another part of the house, the living room for example, there was the aroma of burning fruitwood from the previous evening's fire. The delicate fragrance of the large floral arrangements, ingeniously assembled by the gardener in the orangery, encircled the tables and threw you into the sensual generosity of a Fragonard painting; a jazz record, the trumpet of Dizzy Gillespie or the saxophone of Coltrane, would captivate you as guests drifted between the lounge and large terrace.

In that magnificent salon with deep sofas, windows adorned with heavy curtains, an entire world of objects and paintings could be admired in one glance, but at the same time required an infinite amount of time to be appreciated in detail. There are several levels of understanding articulated in this space, and each of them calls to you for different reasons. This atmosphere is both cozy and inspired, evoking the charm and warmth of an English mansion. It is proof of a refined *savoir vivre* that does not limit itself to decoration as an art form just to be admired, but to be experienced with all of our senses. This experience, because that is what it is, envelopes you and transports you wherever your imagination may take you. The salon is much larger than its physical size, and opens onto endless perspectives far beyond the park seen through the windows.

In the red-orange salon on the rue du Faubourg Saint-Honoré, the same experience is renewed and deeply imprinted on you. What is most striking and appealing are the contemporary pieces that tear themselves away from their time and seamlessly take their place in this ambiance. Everything changes and nothing changes, only the reverie or meditation increases, carried by the grand volume of the room. The tables by Diego Giacometti, laden with books, never cease to charm you with their little perched birds, and the colored neon table by Ron Ferri all fit in perfectly with the Chinese ceramic horses and Balthus's *Le Panier de Cerises*. We would say today that it was a holistic experience.

Henri constantly sought the perfection of the surroundings, of which decoration only represented one aspect. Indeed, I don't think that style as such was very important to him, only to serve him in creating a very comfortable environment. This philosophy on living was in part derived from his background. It is an *art de vivre* typical of a wealthy family of the European Jewish bourgeoisie from which Henri came. This is a class with humanistic values and broad views on society where politics, travel, art, and finance easily mix together. This heritage also came from knowledge he acquired during his childhood from his family: his mother, who was a painter in her youth and had a remarkable eye, and his grandfather and then later his widowed grandmother, who were antiques dealers who traveled across Europe, especially Spain, to offer their Parisian clients the most magnificent pieces of furniture.

**A place for objects, men, artworks, meditation, and spirituality**
At Montfort, and even more in Paris, it felt like many worlds and time periods coincided. A bit like the superposition of clouds: a world of objects, whether alluring or strange, is at your fingertips—along with furniture meant to make one comfortable, and paintings on the wall, another world of contemplation and of escapism, where you could get lost.

As is undoubtedly the case in most of the residences he decorated, it is experi-

encing art in an everyday setting that is exceptional. An intimacy was created with these works that one would not find in a museum where it is separated from all context. There is a natural and ongoing conversation occurring between the artwork and the inhabitant of the space, in which it seemed to me that the roles were reversed, as I understood much later upon reading "What We See Looks Back at Us" by Georges Didi-Huberman. Indeed, as you look at what is in front of you, you slowly start to see what is inside. In this relationship between conversation and contemplation, I really see Henri: very present and at the same time always preserving his vast world with discretion.

**Freedom of tone**

I loved the watercolors of Sam Francis, but was never fond of César's gilded console. But this little game of "J'aime" and "J'aime pas" seems over-simplistic, because together, these pieces contribute to making you leave your comfort zone. The eclectic ensemble worked surprisingly well and created, in their rapprochement, new, challenging spaces.

Henri, who was extremely serious and rigorous in his work, also loved to have fun. He loved to tell jokes that would make everyone feel comfortable and relaxed. He created a very eventful life for himself with a form of assumed socialite hedonism that drove his appreciation for and attraction to important people, sophisticated palaces, the best wines, and high art. . . . But curiously I was never under the impression that he took himself too seriously.

You would find in his home, in the way that he decorated, a tone of joy and freedom that was contagious. His generous way of life mirrored the richness of his interior world and was evident in his talent for creating well-being and grandeur. To explain or to talk about his choices and decisions was not necessary, as with each space he conceived, he was successful and clear in his intent.

Henri never owned anything but artworks, only moveable pieces, which reflected the way he approached life, his way of traveling the world, his way of inventing new solutions tailored to specific people and places.

Never wanting to be a mentor or a teacher, he left us the choice to interpret his legacy, to be inspired by the richness of his inventiveness in mixing art forms, that so many places, as you will discover in this book, testify to.

A view from the interior courtyard into Henri Samuel's Pompeian-red salon at 118, rue du Faubourg Saint-Honoré, Paris.

# AN INTRODUCTION

*I follow instinct and taste, never fashion. I abhor fashion.*

—HENRI SAMUEL

**THE WORLD OF HENRI SAMUEL** is one that has all but vanished. Samuel and his circle dedicated their lives to pursuing and perfecting a refined way of life few today would have the discipline and discernment to achieve. Instant gratification and comfort are now prized above quality and elegance, and self-promotion and social media have rendered privacy almost obsolete. While we are caught up in the whiplash cycle of fast fashion, where trends expire almost as quickly as they are consumed, Samuel and his contemporaries strove for excellence and staying power, operating under the assumption that things should last a generation or more.

Critical to understanding Samuel's approach to decoration is the pivotal role his clients played. It was his charge to provide them with the most perfect ensembles that would serve as foundations for their evolving collections. Samuel enjoyed—and preferred—riffing off his clients' important collections, letting their existing interests, objects, and architecture guide him, rather than beginning with a blank slate. While he never considered himself a collector, he enjoyed meeting contemporary artists and supporting emerging talent. In his own salon on the rue du Faubourg Saint-Honoré, he regarded the furniture he commissioned from these artists as sculpture and separate from the room's otherwise traditional furnishings, which were part of the unchanging ensemble.

Samuel's collaborations with the French branch of the Rothschild family, collectors par excellence, brought him the most professional renown, particularly his work on the magnificent Second Empire Château de Ferrières. As an important interpreter of *le goût Rothschild* in the postwar era, Samuel brought a freshness and restraint to the style's inherently dense opulence. While other decorators, including Geoffrey Bennison, François Catroux, Alain Demachy, Victor Grandpierre, and Renzo Mongiardino also worked with various members of the family, Samuel uniquely worked with all of them and was entrusted with many of their most important properties.

As Nadine de Rothschild affirms, "Henri Samuel was numero uno." Unlike the emotional mises-en-scène of Renzo Mongiardino, Samuel's work adheres to a classical rigor that prevents it from becoming theatrical. This restraint left room for the clients to add their own personal layers over time and Samuel's clients often lived happily with his decoration for decades. That it physically survived that long speaks to the superlative quality of craftsmanship and materials of a Samuel interior.

Samuel, in his eightieth year, sits with two of his beloved dachshunds in his Paris *grand salon*.

Left, top: Samuel led a fast-paced social life, mixing with clients and friends. Here, he is with the couturier Hubert de Givenchy and two female friends aboard a private yacht in the 1960s.

Left, bottom: Samuel entertained frequently at his country house in Montfort l'Amaury. Guests, including a young Yves Saint Laurent, gather on the terrace in the late 1960s.

When the Second Empire style made a resurgence in the go-go '80s, maximalist iterations by Denning and Fourcade and others exploded in popularity. While this younger generation clearly owed a debt to Samuel, their work was less edited and more exuberant, reading to today's eyes as of its time, period pieces. Samuel himself commented, "Today all my young colleagues are throwing themselves into fabric and upholstery, patterned carpets and slipcovers. I have perhaps myself contributed to this revival when I installed the apartment of Hubert d'Ornano a dozen years ago around the furniture and objects belonging to them. It was a fruitful collaboration. But at the same time I could do something completely different for other clients who perhaps had other desires." Indeed Samuel was remarkable for his ease with an array of historical styles, not just one. In a 1985 interview given late in his life, Samuel assessed that a technical education was necessary, but not key, to being a great decorator: "Everything else comes from inside you. You either have the gift or you don't. You're a decorator the way you are anything, with or without the unique genius that can never be taught." Samuel certainly had that innate spark, but his extensive knowledge and study of the decorative arts elevated him to the level of a master.

In researching Samuel's career, I quickly realized that documenting his every project was an impossible feat. There is no telltale attribute in a Samuel-decorated room that immediately gives away its creator. If Samuel's interiors had any signature at all, it was the welcoming ambience he created that brought a sense of comfort to the eye and the body. Samuel expended great effort cultivating interiors as holistic environments, encompassing not just the decoration, but its scents, sounds, and textures. It was this combination of perfect taste and livability that had clients returning for half a century. In the last year of his life, his phone rang constantly with questions and good wishes from longstanding clients such as Prince Sadruddin Aga Khan, Jayne Wrightsman, and several Rothschild baronesses. On the rare occasions a client allowed his or her residence to be photographed, the owner's name was often not mentioned. This discretion and staying in the background suited Samuel just fine. Similarly he was content to direct, not own, the decorating firm of Alavoine et Cie for nearly twenty-five years and only opened his own business at the age of sixty-six when Alavoine was dissolving.

Samuel was by many accounts brilliant at using his love of entertaining as a platform for promotion. His close friend Arthur Aeschbacher commented that there was a cast of business to his fêtes, whose champagne was

Below, left: Client Jayne Wrightsman is served sorbets molded in the form of various flowers in a cake basket, a typically elaborate dish enjoyed by Samuel and his circle.

Below, right: Samuel and client Susan Gutfreund share *l'heure du thé* with the Duc and Duchesse de Mouchy in the late 1980s.

underwritten for a time by Alavoine. It was exclusively through his socializing and circle of acquaintances that Samuel was hired. His apartments and country houses served as representations of his talent, and they came alive at the lunches and dinners he hosted. Salads might be sprinkled with nasturtium and, if he really wanted to dazzle a favored guest, he would serve his prized white strawberries for dessert. A friend recalled, "Henri was a man who paid great attention to the way he received. At his beautiful country house, he had a sommelier and a maître d'hôtel for the picnics. Magnificent tableware, magnificent silver, a very pleasant kitchen and above all a lot of attention to his guests." Figures from the worlds of fashion, literature, music, and politics, and even, on at least one occasion, the Argentinian polo team would mingle at these stylish gatherings.

Samuel lived well, attended to by a butler, cook, and chauffeur, but he remained grounded and modest about his means compared to his über-wealthy clients. "Never mistake yourself for your clients," he told his niece. "I'm not at all a wealthy man and I'm not at all like those whom I serve with pleasure." Eva Samuel continues, "He had an extremely accurate idea of his position." He once told a client that the reason he commissioned contemporary pieces for himself was because he couldn't afford the best of the eighteenth century. However it is also true that Samuel didn't feel the need to own things; he was more interested in living well, being generous, and following his curiosity. Accordingly, Samuel only ever rented his

Below, left: The Samuel family on the Promenade des Anglais in Nice with the Hôtel Negresco in the background, circa 1910. A young Henri holds the hand of his father, Georges.

Below, right: Samuel's mother, Eva, wearing a fashionably waved bob in the 1920s. Samuel and his brother, Édouard, both adored their glamorous mother.

properties. This disinterest in the need to own property seems to have been a family tradition. Samuel looked after his parents and siblings financially and even gave over a wing of his country house to his brother. Generosity was also a motivation behind many of the commissions he gave to artists to create furniture.

Samuel never lost sight of the boundary between client and decorator, and perhaps because his social life was inextricably linked with work, he seldom revealed intimate thoughts. Both friends and family have remarked on how Samuel always maintained his straight posture, elegant dress, and beautiful manners. When faced with a personal question, he would often deflect it with a witticism or laugh. If he kept himself at a remove, he was able to abandon himself to his passion for music and the camaraderie of his adoring dogs—dachshunds and boxers.

"I would like to tell you something little known: Henri was a great music lover. He went to all the major concerts and often had at his table the composers of the group of Five as well as Francis Poulenc, Georges Auric, the pianist Jacques Février, and Henri Sauguet," Aeschbacher notes. Each year Samuel looked forward to the Salzburg music festival and attended concerts in Paris frequently. In later years friend Gilles Muller often accompanied him and remembers that Samuel, who liked to be home and in bed by a quarter to midnight, would fortify himself before a late concert with a hard-boiled egg and a glass of vodka in lieu of dining afterward. Muller notes, "Henri Samuel was an extremely important personality in Paris. He was someone who was invited everywhere and wasn't just thought of as the decorator of the Rothschilds. He was an extremely urbane, polite, attentive man. Everywhere he went, it was a party when he arrived. Today in Paris this kind of worldly life no longer exists. It was a private world. Now if

Above, left: Henri's father, Georges, in military uniform during the First World War. Georges Samuel immigrated to France from Belgium because of the rights the county afforded Jews, and he was proud to fight for his adopted country.

Above, right: Georges Samuel (far right) participating in a theatrical amusement. He enjoyed writing comedic plays.

Henri Samuel as a young boy.

there are parties, it is always linked to business. When Henri celebrated his ninetieth birthday at Maxim's, it was the last beautiful private party that we had in Paris."

Henri Emmanuel Samuel was born on January 26, 1904, in Paris, the first son and middle child of Georges Benjamin Samuel and Eva Level. The Samuels were a successful family of Jewish bankers and merchants, who disseminated throughout Europe, with branches in England, the Netherlands, Belgium, and France. At the age of twenty-three, Samuel's father, Georges, the youngest of fourteen children, left Brussels (to which his father, Louis, had emigrated from Liverpool, England) for France, attracted by its more favorable laws for Jews. Georges proudly became a naturalized French citizen so that he could enlist in the military and serve in the First World War. While Georges ran his own bank, his real pleasure was writing plays and poetry. Speaking seven languages fluently and a Freemason, he enjoyed participating in political debates during which he argued for the leftist ideals of Prime Minister Édouard Herriot.

On December 9, 1900, Georges married Eva, the only child of Emmanuel and Hélène Level. Eva, too, was artistic. She learned to paint with the artist and musée de Carnavelet conservator Georges Cain and even exhibited in the 1892 Salon des Artistes Français. After having children, she refocused her energies on becoming a fashionable woman of society. Eva's mother, Hélène, moved in with the young couple at their large apartment in a *hôtel particulier* at 10, rue Eugène Labiche in the well-heeled sixteenth arrondisement.

The daughter of a prominent rabbi in Mulhouse, Hélène (née Dreyfuss) left Alsace for Paris at the age of sixteen before the region's annexation to Germany in 1871. The Levels owned an antiques shop on the rue Papillon, which Hélène continued to run after her husband's death. Later, after she was fully immersed in running Eva and Georges's household, the antiques business was taken over by her niece's husband, Jacques Lavaillon. Hélène was a beloved figure in the family and a defining influence on her grand-son Henri, who accompanied her on trips to auction houses and antiques galleries. Short, round, and always wearing a wig to hide her thinning hair, she traveled in France and Spain to acquire inventory for her shop. Henri's older sister Manon (born in 1901) recalled, "She was extremely generous. She would keep her most beautiful objects for her family and she would sell these to them at cost. For her, family was everything. She was very lively and cheerful and she liked helping people." In 1912, Eva gave birth to her youngest child, Édouard.

Samuel grew up in the *bonne bourgeoisie*, enjoying a privileged upper middle class upbringing. The family was attended to by several servants

Below, left: Samuel with his older sister, Manon, at the seaside.

Below, right: Samuel with his family, wearing the elaborate fashions of the day, on holiday in the Alps.

who traveled with them when they spent springtime at the Grand Hotel in Cabourg, summers in Nice, and winters in the Alps to ski. His sister, Manon, captured their childhood in a private memoir:

Right up until the departure, everything ... was put under slipcovers. And since vacuum cleaners didn't exist, dust was raised and chased. All this could not be done last minute so we had to live in these decors of pre-vacation. Chandeliers were wrapped and only glowed faintly. Silverware and copper pots disappeared into envelopes made of newspaper. Then started the packing. Piles of linens, clothing, hats and shoes were packed in large heavy leather trunks. White shoes and socks, dresses for the morning, dresses for the afternoon to go on walks, evening dresses to go to the casino. We used to sit on these trunks to close them. Children were allowed to go see the sea but only with a maid

EQUITABLE LIFE BUILDING. NEW YORK. ROTARY PHOTO E.C.

10781–51

(C) IRVING UNDERHILL N.Y

Samuel worked in a New York bank from the age of sixteen to eighteen. During this time, he sent his father a postcard on which he wrote, "A pretty card of New York to my Didiche who writes me such nice letters and of whom I think often. With love, Henry."

or governess. In Belgium at Ostend, the sea was much further away and we used to take a horse carriage to the water. At lunch time, the women, with their hats dressed with flowers, would converse and drink coffee and go from one living room to another in the hotel. Then they would retreat to their rooms to nap. Around 5 o'clock, after a change of dresses, they would go to the casino for tea. In the evening, men would wear smoking jackets and women would be wearing fancy dresses and furs. At the hotel, there were lots of afternoon parties for the children, and costume balls and the Baccarat room where people would come from everywhere. We would also go to Switzerland in the mountains during summer. We would come back looking rested but never tan.

After attending grammar school at the elite Lycée Janson de Sailly, Samuel was given the choice of going to university or entering a career in banking. He chose the latter and on October 24, 1920, at the age of sixteen, he set sail on the S.S. *France* for an internship at a bank arranged by his father. He lived at the Gotham Hotel (now the Peninsula Hotel) on Fifth Avenue and while he soon realized he had little interest in banking, he refined his English and developed an ease with American culture that would serve him well throughout his career. Upon his return to France approximately two years later, he completed his mandatory military service and in 1925, he secured a salesman position at Jansen, one of Paris's premier interior

decoration firms, and quickly climbed the ranks to assist Stéphane Boudin,
one of the principal designers. Manon recalled the frivolous mood of
the time: "After the war, the partying was insane—all we wanted to do was
dance even after the disaster that had just happened. It was the time when
surprise parties were trendy. There were also big balls in large apartments
or in salons rented for the party. Sometimes three hundred people attended, beautiful buffets [were served]. Parents were sent to play bridge, and all
the young people would dance until 5 a.m."

Samuel reflected, "As a young boy at home in Paris, I used to move the
furniture around. It amused my parents. I decorated my room when I was
about 16, putting plain wallpaper on the wall, then painting it. I covered
the chairs in yellow and purple in the Directoire/Empire style. Really, I was
born that way.... I knew very early on that I would become a decorator....
I made model rooms and furnished them, although oddly enough, later on
in life I designed for the stage just once. I was raised by people who appreciated furniture and objects.... My family put no obstacle in the way of my
vocation." For Samuel, the calling of interior decorator was inevitable.

Little is known about Samuel's career between 1930, when he left Jansen,
and the end of the Second World War. In 1933, Georges lost much of his
personal fortune in the Stavinsky affair, a financial scandal that provoked
a major political crisis, and turned to writing political speeches for pay as
well as selling humble wares such as shoe polish to support the family. It is
almost certain that Samuel began supporting his family financially at this
time and would continue to do so for the rest of his life.

At the onset of the Second World War, Samuel was mobilized into the

French army until the 1940 German attack on France. He returned to Paris where he and his parents remained during the Occupation. Eva, Georges, and Hélène stayed in their apartment while Samuel lived in the *chambre de bonne* of his butler, who had left the city (Samuel promptly redecorated the rooms to his taste). While his parents wore the yellow Star of David to designate their Jewish faith as required by the occupying Germans, Samuel did not and is reputed to have made fake papers for himself and others. A family story recounts Samuel's unflappability as the Gestapo passed him on the stairs of his building. When asked where Henri Samuel lived, he told them that they could find him upstairs and continued to descend. Manon's son Fred Lanzenberg remembers Samuel continuing to work as a decorator during the war, calling himself "Monsieur Henri" and visiting clients on his bicycle. After the war, Samuel soon found employment, first with Maison Ramsay followed by the much grander and established Alavoine located in its own building on the avenue Kléber. Over the next twenty-five years, the names of Henri Samuel and Alavoine became interchangeable.

Always in demand, Samuel never had the chance to retire, continuing to work on plum projects, such as Valentino's seventeenth-century Château de Wideville, until the end. Before his death on September 5, 1996, at the age of ninety-two, the decorator was still looking forward. He was planning to move to a new apartment, which he anticipated decorating in a completely new way. As he once said, "I don't look back. I like the times I live in. My only regret is that I never learned to play the piano well."

In his eighties, Samuel regularly flew across the Atlantic Ocean to visit his American clients. He was known to take the Concorde round trip on the same day. Here, he is pictured on a private plane en route to Los Angeles in the late 1980s.

# I:
# THE ART OF THE ENSEMBLIER

*You must get the architecture right before you can decorate. Architecture is like the face's bone structure and decoration is the maquillage.*

—PRINCESS LAURE DE BEAUVAU-CRAON, client and friend of Henri Samuel

The *grand salon* of the Belgian Ambassador's residence in Washington, D.C., features a French classical ensemble. The house—commissioned by Anna Thomson Dodge for her daughter, Delphine—was designed in the early 1930s by architect Horace Trumbauer, with decoration by Alavoine. In 1945, the Belgian Government purchased the property and consulted Alavoine on its refurbishment.

**HARKING BACK TO LOUIS XIV** and his magnificent palace of Versailles, the classic French interior continues today to be revered as a model of style and elegance. During the eighteenth century, all was under the baton of the architect who ensured that each element of the interior was in harmony. A room's design was conceived as a unified whole, with the architectural shell—walls, ceiling, and floor—as the foundation and the furnishings in logical accord.

Henri Samuel's approach to design—that a room was conceived as an ensemble—was formed at Maison Jansen and Alavoine et Cie,[1] two historic decorating firms that revered the classical tradition. The French term "*ensemblier*" was used dominantly in the 1920s and 1930s to refer to today's interior designer, and its root in the word "ensemble" underscores the French tradition that a space should be addressed globally and designed in tandem with all parts considered.[2] To achieve this, the *ensemblier* required both a technical understanding of how to structure interiors and the aesthetic vision to decorate them.[3]

Left, top and bottom: Maison Jansen's two
storefronts on the rue Royale: number six
featured contemporary furniture, reflecting
the latest styles, and number nine offered
historicist and antique pieces. Samuel
began his five years at Jansen working as
a salesman.

Opposite: A glittering mix of
mirror and crystal brings glamor to
the antiques-filled Paris apartment
of fashion designer Coco Chanel,
decorated by Jansen between the
First and Second World Wars.

That the *ensemblier* supplanted the eighteenth-century architect stemmed from the rise of the bourgeoisie after the French Revolution. In the nineteenth century, a burgeoning upper-middle class with new fortunes made in commerce and industrialization became the leading patrons of the fine and decorative arts. While they created a lively consumer market for luxury goods, their taste and needs were much less grand than those of the court of Versailles. It was often the *tapissier* (upholsterer) or the *ébéniste* (furniture maker) who advised on the furnishing and supplied all that a client might need to complete a new interior. Jansen and Alavoine, both founded in the late nineteenth century, developed out of this construct, originating as furniture makers.

Maison Jansen was founded in 1880 by Jan-Hendrik Jansen (known in France as Jean-Henri or Henri), the third son of Hendrik Frederik Jansen, whose Amsterdam firm H. F. Jansen and Sons was known for its high-quality furniture and trims. By 1871, H. F. Jansen had been awarded the royal warrant for supplying furnishings to the Dutch royal family and, within twenty years, its workshops had expanded so that it was the largest furniture manufacturer in Amsterdam. It is not clear if Jean-Henri's Paris enterprise was considered an outpost of his father's business or operated entirely independently at the beginning. Regardless, at the age of twenty-six, he left Amsterdam to begin his new business as an experienced furniture retailer with most likely some capital from his family.

Jean-Henri had an innate flair for promotion, immediately getting attention with flamboyant window displays at Maison Jansen's premises on the fashionable rue Royale. Following the model of his father's firm, he participated in several exhibitions, winning prizes and commissions from illustrious patrons such as King Leopold II of Belgium. Jansen began by offering pieces made in the latest Orientalist and Japonisme fashions, at its retail gallery at 6, rue Royale, but, interestingly, diversified to offer its clients

antiques across the street at 9, rue Royale in an eighteenth-century *hôtel particulier* built for the duc de la Rochefoucauld-Liancourt.[4] Jean-Henri's ambitions resulted in expansion and, between 1905 and 1922, offices were established in Alexandria, Buenos Aires, Cairo, Havana, London, and New York, the latter at a short-lived gallery, in 1915.[5]

With its roster of Café Society clients including Coco Chanel, the Duke and Duchess of Windsor, and Helena Rubinstein, Jansen had a particular reputation for chic by the 1920s. The firm became identified with its stylish handling of eighteenth- and early nineteenth-century-based interiors as formulated by Stéphane Boudin (1888–1967), who joined the firm in 1923 and rose to principal designer by 1930.[6] Boudin had a particularly strong feeling for neoclassicism, which gave a rigor and snappiness to a room. Samuel would later credit Boudin with developing his own taste for the Empire style. Boudin's arrival at Jansen signaled a reorganization of the firm as he, along with two others, bought partnership stakes in the company. This cash infusion undoubtedly helped Jansen recover from its extensive international expansion as well as the toll taken by the introduction of income tax in 1914.[7]

In 1925, Henri Samuel joined Jansen at the age of twenty-one. It was the same year of Paris's Exposition des arts décoratifs et industriels modernes, which promoted modern design, but Samuel did not look to any of the exhibiting designers for his first job. Newly returned from a banking internship in New York and his mandatory military service completed, Samuel was resolved to pursue decoration as a profession. Given the tremendous influence of his maternal grandmother, Hélène Level, who took a young Samuel with her on antiquing expeditions, it is unsurprising that Samuel already had a taste for the traditional and that his first inclination was to seek employment with the carriage trade firms who supplied mainly historicist interiors to the wealthy.[8] Toward the completion of his stint in New York, Samuel unsuccessfully applied to Alavoine for a position on the recommendation of the decorative painter Louis Bouché. Once back in Paris, he found a place with Jansen, where he spent the next five years. "It was then a great house, an institution with branches all over the world. Stéphane Boudin was a specialist of the grand genre, very eighteenth century. The notion of style was very important. It was the great period of historic reconstructions starting from antique *boiserie*, the *ne plus ultra* of decoration,"[9] recalled Samuel.

At the time Samuel joined the firm, Jansen comprised the two rue Royale

Opposite: Two Jansen interiors designed by Stéphane Boudin showcase the firm's use of historical styles. Above is the dining room at The Holme in Regent's Park, London, conceived in the Empire style around 1939 for its owner Audrey Pleydell-Bouverie, sister of the surrealist collector Edward James. Below is the pale blue and silver rococo extravaganza created for Sir Henry Channon at 5 Belgrave Square, London, in 1935. The dining room's paneling was hand-carved in wood and plaster by Jansen's workshop and inspired by the eighteenth-century Hall of Mirrors at the Amalienburg Palace in Munich.

The music room at Cornelius Vanderbilt II's Newport mansion The Breakers exemplifies the taste for French eighteenth-century-style interiors among America's newly moneyed at the turn of the twentieth century. Allard and Sons, a firm later acquired by Alavoine, was hired to carry out the residence's decorative schemes between 1893 and 1895.

retail establishments, along with its own celebrated workshop employing up to seven hundred artisans[10] in a five-story building at 48, rue Saint-Sabin. Cabinetmakers, painters, carvers, carpenters, gilders, bronze workers, and upholsterers were on hand to craft nearly every element of a project. The level of skill was so superlative that reproduction copies of antique furniture made by the firm now command as much as period examples. In addition to stocking the retail boutiques and providing the furnishings for their local projects, the workshop also executed furnishings for the international outposts of the firm. Jansen prized the specialized and highly developed skills of their craftsmen and later invested heavily to keep up training standards as one of the first supporters of the École Camondo, a school founded to train interior designers and artisans in the historical styles.

"I was only at Jansen for five years, but I really learned the business there. For me, there was only Boudin. I owe him a lot. He could be difficult with people who worked for him, but I must say I was one of the very few he respected," Samuel once stated.[11] By all accounts, Boudin was a demanding figure. "When he said he wanted something in one or two days, he expected it to be done in that time.... [He was] very strict," remembers Jansen staff member Albert Ernandez.[12] Boudin himself remarked that, without him, "Jansen would fail because no one would be as strict as I am."[13]

His staff were expected to comport themselves in a highly professional, "masculine" manner. A Jansen designer should be able to socialize easily and hold his own at any table, comporting himself as a social equal to his client, not as a tradesman.[14] However, "it was not proper to overshadow the client," Claude Mandron, a Jansen designer, recalled. "We assisted the individual.... [This] is why you rarely see a period credit assigned to a Jansen interior.... We merely aided."[15] This practice of staying in the background, often anonymous, was one Samuel maintained years after leaving Jansen.

Boudin possessed a meticulous attention to detail that included creating an enormous reference library of historic design. Artists were dispatched around Europe to draw architectural details that were then bound into compendiums for the Jansen designers to consult. For the first two years, Samuel assisted Boudin while learning the technical side of the craft. The practice of creating a reference library was one Samuel himself repeated in his own office. Clients recall paging through these books to select architectural details.[16]

Boudin worked on many projects in England at this time, and Samuel's excellent command of the language would have made him an asset. Samuel quickly graduated to overseeing projects, such as a Vanderbilt residence in New York and the Cleveland residence of department store heir Salmon Halle, who was also the grandfather of future client John Gutfreund.[17] Samuel's nephew Fred Lanzenberg relates that it was his great success as a salesman in the Jansen boutiques that began his career rise. Indeed, Samuel recounted selling a suite of Charles X furniture to William Randolph Hearst that decades later he spotted at the White House. Even without a New York office during this time, Jansen courted and pursued American clients. After the Second World War, Boudin's daughter recalls riding with her father in his Packard and instructed to speak English in hopes of falling into conversation with wealthy Americans.

We are left to speculate why Samuel left Jansen just as it was entering its golden age. Jansen historian James Archer Abbott cites the possibility of tension with Boudin. Samuel's family suggest that he continued to capitalize on his talents selling to wealthy, often American, clients. During the Second World War, Samuel remained in Paris with false papers so that he didn't have to register his address with the local police station or sew the yellow Star of David onto his coat, signifying himself as a Jew. He contin-

Whitemarsh Hall, the baronial residence of Eva and Edward Stotesbury, was built by architect Horace Trumbauer in 1921, with Lord Duveen overseeing the decoration, which was predominately carried out by Alavoine. The woodwork in the sixty-six-foot-long ballroom was designed to showcase the important seventeenth-century Beauvais tapestries Duveen had acquired for his clients.

In 1934, automobile heiress Anna
Thomson Dodge employed the same
team as the Stotesburys for her house
Rose Terrace II in Grosse Pointe Farms,
Michigan—Horace Trumbauer,
Lord Duveen, and Alavoine. In the
breakfast room, Alavoine supplied
Louis XV–style decoration.

Above: The library at Rose Terrace II featured oak boiseries carved by Alavoine's workshops in France. At the end of the room hung a 1932 portrait of Anna Thomson Dodge as Madame de Pompadour (opposite) by artist Gerald Kelly.

ued to work as "Monsieur Henri," with the help of an upholsterer, and visited clients by bicycle.[18]

At some point, most likely immediately following the war, Samuel briefly joined the firm Maison Ramsay, which was founded in 1931 by André Hammel and Louis Seé. Hammel would make a reputation for himself as a decorator and grand *antiquaire* while less is known about Seé, who most likely oversaw the firm's furniture production. The Ramsay boutique was located at 54, rue du Faubourg Saint-Honoré, where it offered a mix of antiques and contemporary furniture, such as cocktail tables of glass and bronze. Jacques Franck was long associated with the firm, working as an in-house decorator through the 1960s. The American heiress Elizabeth Ridgway also worked in some capacity with them in the 1940s when she was Princess Chavchavadze. In the 1960s, André Hammel exhibited under the name of Ramsay at the newly launched Biennale des antiquaires, an exhibition at the Grand Palais in Paris of leading antiques dealers. Ramsay

continued to offer contemporary furniture, including pieces designed by Louis Seé's daughter Françoise, into the 1970s.

Samuel's next association with an established house of decoration commenced around 1946 when he was offered the plum position as manager of Alavoine et Cie, located in a *hôtel particulier* at 42, avenue Kléber.[19] The story of Alavoine is a fascinating one, reputedly tracing back

> through an unbroken succession of family-owned ventures and partnerships to a pioneer group of eighteenth-century craftsmen, members of the Paris guilds (picture-frame carvers, cabinetmakers, furniture makers, *tapissiers*, and so on) who, departing from tradition, organized an archetypal decorating firm. This ancient predecessor of Alavoine appears to have been one of the earliest private organizations in the decorative arts to have provided its clients with a range of services rather than only the products of a single craft. It differed from the historic community of workshops at the Gobelins manufactory in that the latter had been established and maintained under royal subsidy (and were, of course, much larger and more comprehensive).[20]

While this was the history Alavoine presented in the 1960s when it was nearing its end, it can be documented back, from a chain of businesses absorbing businesses, to the 1830s.

The firm began as L. Alavoine et Cie, officially founded in 1887 by the eponymous Lucien Alavoine and his silent partner Édouard Mamelsdorf.[21] Mamelsdorf, a wealthy businessman with interests in the textile trade, first met Alavoine when he employed the firm of Eugène Roudillon to furnish his Paris town house. Eugène Roudillon was an acclaimed *tapissier-ébéniste*[22] known for the superlative quality of his historicist furniture ever since the firm was first recorded in 1844.[23] Their showroom was located at 9, rue Caumartin and employed more than five hundred craftsmen. Mamelsdorf was so taken with Alavoine, the young employee who assisted him, that he encouraged him to start his own business and provided the financing to do so. Alavoine soon bought out Roudillon in 1893, but continued to trade on the cachet of the name by still advertising and marking furniture as "L. Alavoine et Cie (Maison Roudillon)" into the early twentieth century. Martin Becker, who later ran the New York office, noted:

> The carriages of everyone of importance came to the cobblestone courtyard on the rue Caumartin. Alavoine seemed to do almost every

important piece of work that was being done at the time—even the interiors of the palace of the Emperor of Japan. I was told that Alavoine had a beautiful delivery carriage that was well known in Paris. Four superb horses, and the men in livery. Older men told me how magnificent it looked going through the streets of Paris making deliveries. Then the Americans came: Astor, Oelrichs, Berwind, Duke—they all visited Alavoine when they came over to Paris.[24]

Mamelsdorf's enthusiasm for Alavoine can't be underestimated. It was at Mamelsdorf's behest that a New York office open, and in 1893 L. Alavoine and Co. launched at 621 Broadway.[25] The firm's swift success was undeniably related to its fruitful association with Jules Allard et Fils, a celebrated Parisian decorating firm that began, like Roudillon, as a master furniture maker. Alavoine bought the firm after Jules Allard's death in 1907 and, in so doing, were able to keep the important patronage of the palace-building architect Horace Trumbauer, who had worked with Allard for years.

At the end of the nineteenth century, Jules Allard became the decorator par excellence for America's Gilded Age mansions through his affiliation with Richard Morris Hunt and later Lord Duveen. Hunt was the preferred architect of the Vanderbilt family, who were determinedly forging a place in high society through marble and stone. Allard's first American commission was in 1880 for Mrs. William Henry Vanderbilt's boudoir in her house at 640 Fifth Avenue. This was followed by interiors for Cornelius Vanderbilt II including, in 1893, The Breakers, his cottage in Newport, Rhode Island. Here the installation of eighteenth-century boiseries salvaged from the salon of a Parisian *hôtel particulier* was one of the first in a Gilded Age interior and inspired many others to emulate it.[26] A tremendous appetite for French-style interiors in the New World encouraged Allard to open a New York office in 1885. Allard soon realized how difficult it was to create large French-style decors in America as the craftsmanship and knowledge of historical styles and techniques didn't exist. Accordingly, most commissions were made in the Paris workshop and shipped over by boat. By the turn of the twentieth century, America's merchant princes had embraced the fashion set by the Rothschilds for historicist eclecticism, and Allard and Alavoine were at the vanguard of Franco-American taste.

The alliance of Hunt and Allard was a happy one—Hunt was the first American to attend the illustrious École des Beaux-Arts, training under Hector Lefuel, architect to Emperor Napoléon III. In addition to being

trained in French neoclassicism, he also was educated with the belief that
the treatment of interiors should fall under the purview of the architect.
Allard ably understood and carried out Hunt's vision.

After Hunt's death in 1895, Horace Trumbauer, another architect with
a taste for French neoclassicism, continued to build palaces for the newly
moneyed, entrusting Allard and Alavoine with the interiors. "Trumbauer
learned early—probably from examining Hunt's great palaces in Newport
and elsewhere—to depend for the detailed design and execution of his
superb French interiors upon Jules Allard et Fils and Lucien Alavoine et
Cie,"[27] concluded James T. Maher in *The Twilight of Splendor: Chronicles of
the Age of American Palaces.* Clients such as James B. Duke, Senator William
Clark, Frank Woolworth, and Hamilton Rice entrusted Trumbauer and his
decorators to build their princely palaces.

At the same time that Allard became part of Alavoine, the firm received
other high-profile commissions such as furnishing the lobby and Oak
Room of the new Plaza Hotel in New York. Newport Preservation Society
curator Paul Miller observes, "I believe Alavoine were largely seen, until
1907, as secondary suppliers and sub-contractors... only emerging as
deluxe decorators following the merger with Allard."[28] When Alavoine
bought out Allard, it immediately acquired its reputation and clientele.[29]

In the meantime, in addition to contributing decor and furnishings to
ocean liners including the SS *Atlantique* and the SS *Normandie,* the Paris office also continued to support and supply the New York branch of
Alavoine. In the early 1930s, at the height of the Depression, Alavoine
was kept engaged by Dodge automobile heiress Anna Thomson Dodge.[30]
Widowed and one of the wealthiest women in the country, Dodge commissioned Horace Trumbauer to replace her Jacobethan-style house, Rose
Terrace, in Grosse Pointe Farms, Michigan, having been convinced by her
art adviser Lord Duveen that she needed a more suitable setting for her
collections. Rose Terrace II would be one of Trumbauer's last projects and
was considered an exceptional iteration of French neoclassicism. The "*petit
palais*" was modeled after—but larger than—Miramar, the Newport cottage
Trumbauer designed for Eleanor and George Widener.[31] For the interiors,
Duveen swept Anna off to Europe to shop for boiseries and other antique
furnishings, which were then installed by Alavoine. Duveen, Trumbauer,
and Alavoine had also collaborated on Whitemarsh Hall, the magnificent
Main Line Philadelphia Georgian-style residence of Eva Stotesbury, who
for a brief time was the mother-in-law of Anna Dodge's daughter, Del-

phine. When Delphine married her second husband, Raymond Baker, in 1928, Anna commissioned Trumbauer to build a thirty-room house in Washington, D.C., as a wedding present, with Alavoine providing the decoration. In the meantime, Delphine's first husband and Stotesbury's son, James Cromwell, would later marry Doris Duke, whose Fifth Avenue childhood home was also a Trumbauer-Alavoine creation.

Alavoine enjoyed long-term, multigenerational relationships with their clients. These connections were still intact when Samuel started at Alavoine around 1946. One of his first projects was decorating the Paris house Doris Duke gave to her second husband, Porfirio Rubirosa, on the rue de Bellechasse in 1947. Samuel would also consult on the Washington, D.C., Delphine Dodge Cromwell Baker Godde house after it was purchased in 1945 by the Belgian Embassy, who hired Alavoine to complete their original plans.[32]

The American market was essential to Alavoine's long success, with the New York office driving much of the firm's business. However, soon after Samuel became head of Alavoine in Paris[33] after the Second World War, the acclaim the firm received would be for its work in France, while the New York office quietly continued to work with generations of the same families until its closing in 1964. At Jansen, Stéphane Boudin ended his career with a grand finale—the redecoration of the Kennedy White House. After his death in 1967, Samuel inherited many of Boudin's most faithful clients[34] including Jayne and Charles Wrightsman. The flame of both firms flickered and dimmed in the 1960s. In 1970, at the age of sixty-six, Samuel would finally open his own business: Henri Samuel Décorateur. No matter where he worked, Samuel dedicated himself for over seventy years to his profession, elegantly described by a contemporary: "The decorator will always think of his art as a human art above all, and that his efforts will create a setting of joy and love."[35]

Stéphane Boudin of Jansen was commissioned to decorate areas of the White House, including the Yellow Oval Room, during the Kennedy administration. Jayne Wrightsman introduced Jacqueline Kennedy to the decorator in 1959.

# II:
# RESTORATION

*Outraged Paris! Broken Paris! Martyred Paris! . . . France returns to Paris, to her home. She returns bloody but quite resolute.*

—CHARLES DE GAULLE, on the liberation of Paris, August 25, 1944

Henri Samuel strategically used bursts of emerald green to play off a folding screen painted by Édouard Vuillard in the salon of Cuban business-man Jacques Abreu, around 1960.

**AFTER THE SECOND WORLD WAR,** the people of Paris found themselves psychologically, physically, and financially bereft after four years of German occupation. Broke and battered, the city would take years to recover, with rations continuing into 1949. An American visitor in 1947 noted, "The food scarcity was acute, the cost of living was astronomical, and a pall of cynicism and futility hung over the inhabitants. Everywhere you went, you sensed the apathy and bitterness of a people corroded by years of enemy occupation."[1] That same year came a bold green shoot of renewal when couturier Christian Dior launched his defiantly optimistic New Look. The instantly acclaimed fashion silhouette featured a hyper-feminine wasp waist, set off by a voluminous skirt whose yardage requirements thumbed its nose at fabric restrictions. Paris's international reputation for style once again helped bring fame and fortune back to its banks.

As Parisian life slowly rebounded, a mood of nostalgia took hold, along with a desire to restore the city to its former glory. The nation and its leading private citizens considered it a moral duty to revitalize its historic cultural institutions in an effort to reignite a sense of pride.[2] Classic French decoration was very much in fashion in France and abroad, and the decorating firms Alavoine, Jansen, and Carlhian[3] were considered Paris's "Big Three," according to the esteemed arts magazine *Apollo*.[4] By 1947, Henri

Samuel was ensconced as manager of Alavoine's Paris office, a position he
embraced with gusto. He was an ideal choice: trained by their competitor
Jansen and with the connections and personality to bring in business. Client getting was a subtle art and came from socializing rather than advertising. Samuel later reflected, "I know all my clients through my life outside
work. I never propose anything to people. People come to me." Commissions rolled in: by the mid-1950s, Alavoine had already provided decoration for the luxury hotels George V, in Paris, and the Hôtel de Paris, in
Monte Carlo; Maxim's upstairs dining room; President Charles de Gaulle's
private railway car; and the ocean liner S.S. *Liberté*.[5]

Entertaining was Samuel's calling card, and he decorated his residences as
a showcase for his work. Potential clients experienced his spaces as a way
of life, in an elegant symbiosis of decoration and lifestyle, which Samuel
constantly sought to perfect for his guests' pleasure. Samuel rented both
an apartment in an eighteenth-century house on the Left Bank's rue du
Bac and Saint Vigor, a country house just outside of Paris in Viroflay. After
transforming them into refined examples of his decorating vision, the
parties began, underwritten by Alavoine.[6] In her society column for the
*Philadelphia Inquirer*, Gloria Braggiotti Etting recorded one such occasion
during a trip to Paris in July 1949:

> Paris is bustin' out all over with a frenzy of activity and we've been
> walking on air ever since we landed.... Now that the telephones no
> longer leave you hanging in suspense and the taxi drivers don't ask
> you what direction you are heading before they allow you to hop in, as
> in the early post-war days, life is one mad stream of merging engage-
> ments.... At a garden party lunch we attended at the country house of
> Henri Samuel at Viroflay just outside Paris, there wasn't a woman who
> didn't sparkle with a genuine piece of jewelry even though she wore
> the simplest cotton dress. Madame Arturo Lopez, dark and exotic, had

a blackamoor of rubies, diamonds and emeralds clipped on her saffron linen dress. Madame Louis Cartier wore a white silk crochet cap pierced by a gold bamboo bar pin.[7]

Marie Pierre "Mapie" de Toulouse-Lautrec (the sister of novelist Louise de Vilmorin), *Vogue* editor Nicolas de Gunzburg, and Porfirio Rubirosa (newly divorced from Doris Duke) counted among the "other guests lolling on the shaded lawns, cooled by a central fountain, or sitting at tables under arches of cerise rambling roses." Rubirosa was a recent client of Samuel's. Doris Duke called in Alavoine, whom she considered the family decorators, to outfit a seventeenth-century house at 36, rue de Bellechasse that she bought from Princess Chavchavadze in 1947 as a wedding present for her new husband. The first two floors were decorated with Louis XV and XVI pieces, with a boxing ring and full bar installed on the top floor.[8]

Etting continued to describe the day that was captured by society photographer André Ostier's lens, "We roamed through every precious room of this little Louis Fifteenth country house—Palace to us—once the gift of Louis Fifteenth to his nanny, Madame Mercier." Saint Vigor was indeed a magnificent house. Its elaborate classical architectural detail required little decoration to make an impression, in contrast to Samuel's second country house.

By 1952, Samuel had left Viroflay for Montfort l'Amaury, an hour's drive west of Paris, where Christian Dior and Mexican silver heir and aesthete Carlos de Beistegui also had houses. While Samuel opted for a more contemporary tone in the city, with modern art and a smoking room that had

**Henri Samuel, Saint Vigor**

Samuel's residences were important showcases of his work. Opposite and above, left: Two views of the main salon.

Above, right: The house's entrance hall with porcelain stove.

**Henri Samuel, La Bouteriez**

By 1952, Samuel was renting a country house in Montfort l'Amaury, which he decorated as a "maison de famille." Opposite: This small sitting room, which leads to the main salon, is hung in ivory percale and framed by the same floral border used on the salon's curtains.

Above: The house was in a park-like setting dotted with gardens.

a sculptural plastic wallcovering, his country house La Bouteriez, which he rented from the writer Jacques de Lacretelle, was all about the romance of the past. Arts journal *Connaissances des arts* enthused, "The dernier cri of good taste at the moment is to create decoration that reconstitutes the atmosphere of 'our grandmother's house in the country' or 'family house' where generations have accumulated handsome furniture of all periods. . . . The house decorator Henri Samuel has arranged for himself . . . is a ravishing example."[9]

This eighteenth-century dwelling, distinguished by its rustic high-pitched tile roof, was in a bad state of repair when Samuel took it on. He first addressed structural elements, shifting fireplaces and installing boiseries. To create a relaxed, modern feel, cotton fabrics rather than heavy and expensive brocaded and woven silks were selected for even the reception rooms. In one salon, the curtains were made of ivory percale printed with gray vermicelli inspired by Marie Antoinette's own in the Trianon, and three identical tufted sofas were covered in bright blue poplin. The centerpiece of the house was the *grand salon*, interpreted by Samuel as a winter gar-

**Henri Samuel, La Bouteriez**

Left: Samuel's talents as a colorist are on display in the exuberant winter garden room.

Above: The dining room, opening to the terrace and the garden, features an architectural Directoire wallpaper and woodwork that has been faux-painted to look like mahogany. Samuel sits center right with Madame Serge Landeau to his left; Arthur Aeschbacher at the head of the table; Countess Marie Pierre "Mapie" de Toulouse-Lautrec wearing her signature hat; and Cecil Everly sitting opposite.

den, an indoor salon-cum-conservatory made popular by Napoléon's niece Princesse Mathilde in the 1850s. This moment of Second Empire fantasy may have been inspired by the nineteenth-century Rothschild châteaux of Ferrières and Lafite that Samuel was currently restoring. Tropical scenic wallpaper was amplified by potted palms and a vigorously floral-patterned carpet. An exuberant Napoléon III *confidante* tufted in tomato-red satin furthered the intoxicating hothouse ambience. Throughout the house Henri mixed Second Empire–style furnishings with Louis XVI ones, incorporating all the modern conveniences such as comfortable seating and proper lighting. The result was a mise-en-scène that appeared to have evolved over generations rather than being instantaneously installed. Visitors to Henri's residences consistently exclaimed how at ease and welcomed they felt in his spaces.

**Henri Samuel, La Bouteriez**

In the salon, strategically placed mirrors and views of the garden enliven the gray-painted boiseries.

Samuel's romantic approach to country house decoration reached a high point in his collaboration with Louise de Vilmorin, a woman of letters and lovers. Close to Viroflay, where Samuel and his extended family gathered during his childhood, was Vilmorin's own family house, the Château de Vilmorin in Verrières-le-Buisson. The seventeenth-century manor house was acquired in 1815 by the Vilmorin family, who amassed a fortune cultivating seeds. Successive generations enlarged the house and expanded the gardens to include a private arboretum. Verrières was precious to Vilmorin and, during her time as *châtelaine*, many artists and intellectuals found their way to her Sunday salons.

Jean Cocteau, who was a guest for several months while finishing *La difficulté d'être*, waxed poetic in his journal, "I find in this cold moonlight the house I adore, the one Charles Beistegui dreams of and that his fortune will never obtain. A house like this is made of a long series of a family's

**Henri Samuel, La Bouteriez**
A Brighton Pavilion chinoiserie influence
permeates the master bedroom.

obsessions of the soul. Nothing is beautiful. Everything is beautiful."[10]
Flush from the proceeds of her 1951 novella *Madame de*, which was soon
optioned by Hollywood, Vilmorin enlisted Samuel to help her refresh
what would famously be dubbed the Salon Bleu. Its classical allure and
nostalgic atmosphere became intimately linked with her persona to the
point that she later took full credit for its decoration. For Samuel, this was
high praise.

The Salon Bleu derived its name from the blue-and-white cotton print
used almost exclusively throughout the room. When it was first published
in 1953 by *Maison et Jardin*, the magazine acclaimed, "This fabric, without
pomp or pretension, evokes the charms of summer and private pursuits."[11]
The floral sprays and borders of Batik, the simple cotton print still pro-
duced by Georges Le Manach, the French fabric house founded in 1829,
reminded Samuel of blue-and-white porcelain. It was one he had used
previously and would continue to use, particularly in bedrooms. *Maison
et Jardin* also commented on Samuel's unconventional pairing of blue
and black, embodied in the six black lacquer tables inset with Japanese
blue-and-white porcelain tiles that he made to Vilmorin's specifications. A
symmetrical placement of furniture gave structure to the scheme, loosened
by the occasional nineteenth-century pouf or *confidante*. Tabletops were
densely arranged with collections of malachite vessels, silver figures of
birds and fishes, and other bibelots. The large Turkish carpet in tones of
pink and ivory gave a warm glow to the décor.

For war hero and defense minister General Pierre Billotte and his wife,
Sybil, Samuel created a stylish version of a cozy and old-fashioned *maison
de famille* at the Château de Bois-Feuillette. In the dining room, the walls
and curtains were made of a traditional toile de Jouy print, but the color-
way of gray on white paired with the punchy yellow seat upholstery was
anything but dowdy. Samuel paid homage to the general's esteemed military career with a striped, tented dressing room evocative of Napoléon's
campaign tents.[12]

Sought after for his chic handling of historical styles, Samuel was often
asked to infuse a modern building with the spirit of the eighteenth century.
For industrialist Michel Bolloré and his family, he took on the large project
of an entire house near the Bois de Boulogne, whose construction had
been halted by the Second World War. When Bolloré purchased it in the
mid-1950s, the building was essentially a shell with a roof and modern exterior. The couple asked Samuel to combine the elegance of the Louis XV

**Louise de Vilmorin,
Château de Verrières**

Around 1953, Samuel decorated the
Salon Bleu of novelist Louise de
Vilmorin at her family's house in
Verrières-le-Buisson. The name of
the room is derived from the color of
the cotton print Batik, which is used
throughout the space.

**Louise de Vilmorin,
Château de Verrières**

The novelist sits at work in the Salon
Bleu, surrounded by her collections of
silver animals, malachite objects, and
ancestral works of art.

Right: In the 1950s, Samuel threw a ball at the Musée Grévin wax museum in Paris. A Brazilian band from Paris's most exclusive nightclub played samba music for the evening.

Opposite: For the ball's decoration, Samuel borrowed a nineteenth-century circular sofa, centered by a towering arrangement of palm fronds and flowers, from the Château de Ferrières to create a Second Empire ambience.

Above: Samuel poses with wax figures of the recently crowned Queen Elizabeth II and her consort, Prince Philip, at the Musée Grévin.

and XVI periods with contemporary comfort. A classic ensemble would serve as a background to their modern art collection of works by Fernand Léger, Georges Braque, and Pablo Picasso. To let the clear colors of the art stand out, Samuel kept the walls a neutral color. Even the bronze staircase, copied from a Louis XV original belonging to another client,[13] had a stone-colored carpet runner so that a large Constantin Macris abstract oil painting remained the focal point of the entrance hall. In the *grand salon* where the most important pieces of the collection were hung, champagne-hued silk covered the walls. Samuel often chose this color when he wanted to showcase a strong painting collection.[14]

For Samuel and his circle, postwar Paris was a whirl of constant social activity. It was also the era of the ball, a private large-scale party organized around a theme. Samuel attended many, including the Baron de Redé's legendary Bal Oriental. When it was his turn to reciprocate, his selection of the Musée Grevin as the festivity's site was perfectly aligned with the Proustian mood of the day. Founded in 1882, it is one of Europe's oldest wax museums with hundreds of likenesses of both personages from the history of France and modern-day celebrities. Samuel transformed the museum's main spaces with potted palms and a circular sofa from the Château de Ferrières as the centerpiece. Long damask-draped buffet tables held tower-

ing ormolu candelabras and refreshments. While the surroundings were nineteenth century, the party itself was of the moment. Charlie Chaplin and Lauren Bacall were among the attendees who enjoyed the Brazilian orchestra booked for the evening from the most fashionable high-society nightclub, *L'éléphant blanc* in Montparnasse.[15]

Around this time, Samuel created his only set design for the theater. It was for the 1955 production of *Aux innocents les mains pleines* (Fortune to fools) by André Maurois performed at the Comédie-Française. The one-act play based on a proverb was the first (and also the only) play written by Maurois, acclaimed for his literary biographies of Percy Bysshe Shelley, Marcel Proust, and others. Directed by Jacques Charon, actresses Hélène Perdrière and Lise Delamare were costumed in Balenciaga and set off by the cerise pleated-silk *petit salon* designed by Samuel.

Samuel's masterful handling of classicism in a modern way convinced several Portuguese businessmen to make the decorator their top choice to design Lisbon's new deluxe hotel. In the years during and following the war, Lisbon had become a popular departure point for crossing the Atlantic. Prime Minister António de Oliveira Salazar, who was focused on attracting international tourism to the country, was intent that the city needed

Below: Samuel chose Louis XIII–style furnishings and simple English oak paneling for the salon of clients Prince and Princess Sadruddin Aga Khan in the late 1950s. The publication *Connaissances des Arts* called the result "almost modern."

Opposite: For entrepreneur Michel Bolloré's Paris house, decorated in 1958, Samuel selected neutral backgrounds to emphasize the important modern art collection.

**General Pierre Billote,**
**Château de Bois-Feuillette**

Opposite: In the dining room, Samuel plays with pattern, echoing the Aubusson carpet's medallions in the cotton toile de Jouy print of the walls and curtains.

Above, left: In Madame Billote's bedroom, a collection of rare eighteenth-century Chinese flowers hand-painted on rice paper hangs on the pink-painted boiseries.

Above, right: The gray-painted salon is brimming with flowers, from the floral dark brown–ground carpet to the vases filled by Madame Billotte with dahlias.

a grand hotel suitable for receiving foreign dignitaries. In 1953, a group of ten investors committed itself to building a modern hotel that "should provide luxury, and comfort, dignify the city and, above all, honour the nation."[16] In the nearly six ensuing years, the most talented Portuguese artists and artisans were selected to create site-specific tapestries, murals, and more, rendering the hotel a veritable museum of contemporary art. Samuel was tasked with designing the most prestigious areas of the hotel: the Salão Almada Negreiros, the hotel's sprawling lobby named after one of Portugal's leading artists who designed three centaur-themed tapestries for the space, and the restaurant Varanda. Samuel enlisted Lucien Donnat, a French interior designer living in Lisbon, to manage the project. The result, unveiled in 1959, was a sophisticated and show-stopping fusion of Louis XVI and Art Deco.[17] During this same time, the French embassy in Portugal commissioned Samuel to bring warmth to the cavernous ambassador's residence in the Palácio Marquês de Abrantes.[18]

Extolling its history was an important part in balming France's wartime wounds. Versailles, an important symbol of greatness for the country, found an indefatigable champion in Gérald Van der Kemp. Upon becoming Versailles's chief curator in 1953, Van der Kemp found the palace "disgusting, empty and dead" and announced that it must be brought back to

A current view of the lobby of the Hotel Ritz in Lisbon, Portugal, designed by Samuel in the late 1950s. Three large centaur-themed tapestries by the artist José de Almada Negreiros were commissioned specifically for the space.

life and be made as beautiful as it was during the days of the *ancien régime* and Napoléon. Van der Kemp was a fundraising force, attracting primarily private donations from Americans as well as notable contributions from the French Rothschild and David-Weill families to support the epic restoration. Van der Kemp's American wife, Florence Harris, whom he was introduced to by Samuel, devoted herself to assisting his efforts.

Samuel recalled:

> I worked with a museum for the first time, in 1957, at Versailles, thanks to the friendship of Gérald Van der Kemp, who asked me to reinstall an important ensemble of paintings, sculptures, and watercolors from the Empire period. How to present these works? Rather than resorting to, once again, white, gray or beige everywhere, we preferred to upholster the rooms with the sateen printed with all the motifs from the silk factories ordered by the Emperor. It made a grand effect and the paintings were remarkably enhanced in an ambience that evoked the wonder of the imperial residences. Thereafter, it was entrusted to me to do all the draperies and furniture of the Grand Trianon.[19]

In 1963, at the urging of Minister of Cultural Affairs André Malraux, Charles de Gaulle ordered the restoration of the Grand Trianon so it could be used as guest quarters for visiting foreign heads of state in one wing and a private living and working suite for the French president in the Trianon-sous-Bois wing, a later section of the building added in 1708 to house members of the royal family. Guests would be received and congregate in the Trianon's main reception room and the Cotelle Gallery, which linked the Grand Trianon to the Trianon-sous-Bois wing. The restoration itself was completed between 1965 and 1966.

Built for Louis XIV by architect Jules Hardouin-Mansart as a retreat from the rigors of court life, the Trianon's contents were stripped during the Revolution and it languished empty until it became one of Napoléon's official residences. Because it was impossible to re-create any kind of eighteenth-century furnishing plan, Van der Kemp made the decision to interpret the interiors as they were in Napoléon's day with the exception of the paintings, which were reassembled as they were originally hung under Louis XIV. Curator Denise Ledoux-Lebard created an inventory of all the furniture and objets assembled by Napoléon in the Grand Trianon to replace the furniture sold off during the Revolution, and researched the original textiles, many of which were conserved at the Mobilier National,[20]

After the Second World War, the French government sought Samuel's assistance in refurbishing their embassy in Portugal, the historic Palácio de Abrantes. In the imposing *grand salon*, he created several seating groups with Empire-period chairs covered in a pale green satin.

At the behest of Versailles curator Gérald Van der Kemp, Samuel consulted on the restoration of the interiors of the Grand Trianon between 1965 and 1966. In the Mirror Room, one of the largest reception rooms, Samuel oversaw the creation of the new curtains, from the weaving of the silk to their draping and installation.

so they could be copied. Under Ledoux-Lebard's direction, Samuel studied the original sketches from the museum's archives to create accurate facsimiles of the curtains and upholstery. Ledoux-Lebard wrote:

> Everything was done as meticulously and faithfully as possible to return this palace where Napoléon made frequent and long stays, periods very important in his private life, to the exact decor in which he passed rare moments of respite between his campaigns or travels. The Emperor desired furnishings less sumptuous than the other palaces and, although refined, more in accord with his taste for simplicity. More than ever, the request most often found in communications and letters to his stewards was: "Make it simple, it is for the Emperor."[21]

Samuel was also entrusted with decorating the Van der Kemps' own private apartment located in the Dufour Pavilion, a seventeenth-century wing of the palace. The residence was used to entertain prospective donors, and its decoration needed to convey French high style. Florence's inherited

**Gérald and Florence Van der Kemp, Dufour Pavilion**

Opposite: Samuel chose a vibrant sapphire blue for the walls and curtains in the *grand salon* of the Van der Kemps' apartment at Versailles, which was decorated around 1967.

Above: Yellow moiré silk walls set off Madame Van der Kemp's inherited English antiques, which she had shipped over from her native America.

**Gérald and Florence Van der Kemp, Dufour Pavilion**

Left: Samuel shows off the art of the French upholsterer in the dining room. The walls and curtains are hung with cotton printed to look like Lyonnais silk woven for the Empress Joséphine. The dining chairs are upholstered in blue velvet embroidered in gold.

Opposite: A cotton printed with roses, copied from a silk ordered by Louis Philippe for the Élysée Palace, is used throughout Madame Van der Kemp's bedroom.

Sheraton-style furniture was also incorporated in the rooms. In 1967, *Maison et Jardin* commented on the bold colors inspired by the Louis XIV era and the perfection of every detail of the upholstery: "The noble beauty and the historical details of this apartment don't prevent the feeling of exceptional comfort and warmth."[22] Signature Samuel touches that kept the formal scheme fresh included upholstering the dining room walls in a Mulhouse cotton that reproduced the pattern of a Lyon silk woven for the Empress Joséphine.

While working at Versailles was a milestone in his career, it was Samuel's restoration of private palaces that would bring him the most acclaim. The French branch of the Rothschild family wanted to restore several of its illustrious estates, and it was to Samuel they turned.

# III:
# LE GOÛT
# ROTHSCHILD

*Kings couldn't afford this. It could only belong to a Rothschild!*

—WILHELM I, KING OF PRUSSIA, upon seeing the Château de Ferrières

**Château Lafite**

*Le goût Rothschild* has its foundation in the opulent eclecticism of the Second Empire, when Baron James de Rothschild established himself as France's foremost banker.

**OPULENT, OLD-WORLD, AND RICHLY LAYERED,** the style named after one of the most prominent international banking families telegraphs superabundance. Often imitated, *le goût Rothschild* is difficult to duplicate as every element must be superlative. Baron Guy de Rothschild described it as "an atmosphere that is found in most of the homes inhabited by members of my family: a Napoléon III decor, personalized not only by all sorts of objets d'art but above all by a sense of comfort and intimacy which intermingles furniture, flowers, plants, family photographs, precious miniatures and rare books."[1] Baronne Nadine de Rothschild, who had to adjust to the expectations demanded of this grand lifestyle when she married Baron Edmond, noted: "*Le style Rothschild* doesn't just refer to the decoration of houses, the subtle alliance of comfort with museum pieces. The Rothschild style is also a way of living, of receiving, pushed to perfection at the homes of all the members of the family."[2]

Essential to the style is the prominence of collections. It has been said that when a Rothschild begins a collection, he finishes with a museum.[3] According to Rothschild traditions, explains the baronne, it is important not only

**Château de Ferrières**

Built between 1854 and 1862 for
Baron James de Rothschild, the
château was restored one hundred
years later by the Baronne Guy de
Rothschild after German soldiers
had occupied it during the Second
World War.

to safeguard but also to enrich the collection one has inherited. Old-master
paintings, royal eighteenth-century French furniture, and Renaissance
bronzes, representing a multiplicity of historical periods and national origins, were a few of the categories collected during the nineteenth century
and augmented by successive generations.[4] During the Second World War,
the family, as prominent Jews and renowned collectors, were targeted by
the Germans, and many of their French properties were seized and looted.
Following the liberation, it was a matter of pride and defiance to reclaim
and painstakingly restore their properties. It was Henri Samuel whom
several members of the family entrusted to sympathetically breathe new
life and glory into these residences.

The family's fortune originated with Mayer Amschel Rothschild, banker
to the German court in the 1760s. His five sons, often referred to as "the
five arrows," expanded the family's position and wealth by each setting up
business in a different European center of commerce: Frankfurt, London,
Naples, Paris, and Vienna. The blueprint of the Rothschild style originates
back to the mid-nineteenth century, when members of the family built
their first private palaces. It was this period that created a template for

future newly rich merchant princes, including Vanderbilts and Morgans, to emulate. Historian Bruno Pons elaborates:

> Two important aspects seem to need emphasizing. Firstly the Rothschilds, through the links between the various members of the family and the well-known endogamy practiced between the different branches connected to any one country, were to internationalize the attraction of French interiors. Above all, they would give credit to the idea that contemporary residences would be enobled by antique décors, which would also correspond to the enobling of new arrivals in the society of the time.[5]

By the 1850s, the Rothschilds were the world's wealthiest family,[6] and their building was in full swing. The taste for eclecticism that guided their collecting also informed the interior decoration of their houses. A preference for French historicist rooms can be discerned by the 1860s in the English and French branches of the family due in large part to the burgeoning resale market of French boiseries salvaged from seventeenth- and eighteenth-century town houses and châteaux. Swathes of *ancien-régime* houses were demolished by Baron Haussmann's rezoning of Paris between 1853 and

American soldiers recover art looted by the Germans during the Second World War, including an eighteenth-century portrait of a lady (far right) from the Rothschild collection.

1870 and, in 1860, what historian John Harris has described as a watershed for preserving architectural salvage, the seventeenth-century Château de Bercy was razed.[7] This was the last fully furnished château within the limits of Paris to survive the Revolution. An auction of its contents, including the architectural boiseries, attracted Lord Hertford (founder of what is now the Wallace Collection), the Empress Eugénie, and Ferdinand de Rothschild, who was in the midst of planning Waddesdon Manor in Buckinghamshire, England. A quintessential Rothschild interior of this period featured an eighteenth-century architectural shell composed of mixed and matched period boiseries (completed with copywork), overlaid with nineteenth-century upholstery and the owner's collections of paintings and objets.

In 1850 Baron Mayer de Rothschild, from the English branch, commissioned Joseph Paxton, then at work on the acclaimed Crystal Palace exhibition hall, to design a Jacobethan-style house to showcase his collections. While the resulting Mentmore Towers (also in Buckinghamshire) paid homage to the Tudors and Stuarts, it also featured the latest in technology and comfort including plate-glass windows, central heating, and a great hall with a glazed ceiling. Inside, two prevailing styles dominated: certain reception rooms, including the great hall, featured a composite of Renaissance-style architecture, conjuring the idea of a neo-Medici prince, while in more feminine rooms a lighter historicist French treatment was employed.

Mayer's uncle James was so impressed that he hired Paxton to build "another Mentmore, but twice as large" in Ferrières-en-Brie, France. Baron James, the youngest of the five sons, arrived in Paris in 1811 to capitalize on France's need to pay indemnities after the Napoleonic Wars. Described as "short, ugly and proud" by the Marechal de Castellane, the "Grand Baron" soon became the country's most powerful banker and showed just as much determination at socializing, with his wife (and niece), Betty, becoming one of Paris's most prominent hostesses.

Like Mentmore, Ferrières has a two-story square plan with a three-story tower at each of the four corners, conceived in a composite of fifteenth-century styles, from English Tudor to Italian Renaissance. The result was deemed neither avant-garde nor particularly elegant, but magnificent by virtue of its enormity. It was planned as a house for entertaining and, in addition to the public reception rooms, featured eighty guest bedroom suites. On December 16, 1862, Napoléon III graced the house's inaugural gala.

Rothschild historian Pauline Prévost-Marcilhacy notes that "among French

**Château de Ferrières**

The grand hall was copiously furnished in the nineteenth century with over-upholstered furniture, potted palms, and sculpture. After its restoration, Baron and Baronne Guy de Rothschild kept it sparingly furnished.

**Château de Ferrières**

Opposite and above: Two views of the dining room featuring richly carved neo-Renaissance-style oak boiseries. An elaborate chimneypiece was removed to allow room for the set of important seventeenth-century polychrome leather hangings, which previously hung in the Salon Bleu.

châteaux of the nineteenth century, Ferrières occupies an exceptional place for it wasn't conceived by the Grand Baron as simply a place of residence, but as a total work of art where work of great quality from past centuries exist side by side."[8] The artist Eugène Lami, who had just finished decorating the private suites of the Château de Chantilly for the duc d'Aumale,[9] was entrusted to oversee the interior schemes and immediately set off to Venice with Baronne Betty for inspiration. A rich diversity of materials and treatments abounded while the furnishings reflected an uncontained eclecticism.

The ambitious decorative scheme called for specialist artisans, particularly sculptors, placing the Grand Baron as a competitor to Napoléon III himself in engaging available talent to carry out the designs. By choosing contemporary sculptors instead of searching for and designing around antique examples, Lami was free to realize any vision he might have. The Grand Baron's son Alphonse completed the house's decoration, incorporating his own taste for eighteenth- and nineteenth-century French fine and decorative arts, which aligned with the nationalistic mood after France's defeat in the Franco-Prussian War in 1870, during which Ferrières was occupied for the first time by the Germans.[10]

**Château de Ferrières**

Above and opposite: The Salon Bleu was Guy and Marie-Hélène de Rothschild's favorite room in the newly restored château. Blue Turquin marble columns separate the four corners of the room into more intimate seating areas.

The centerpiece of the house was its spectacularly scaled hall, following the tradition of the English "Great Hall." It measured 60 feet high and 120 feet long and was copiously furnished with plush upholstered pieces, potted palms, and more. Baron Guy recalled in his 1985 memoir *The Whims of Fortune*:

> This was the very heart of Ferrières. Two stories high, it was surrounded on the first floor by reception rooms, various drawing rooms, dining rooms, and games rooms, while the upper floor was reserved for the private apartments.... Reminiscent of the Italian loggias for serenading musicians, it also permitted the guests to cast a discreet eye on what was going on downstairs, because the main hall served as the principal living room.... In the middle of the main hall was a circular couch from the centre of which a marble column seemed to spring, surmounted by an 18th-century clock that represented Atlas carrying the world on his shoulders. German armor, Italian sculpture, Flemish tapestries, Napoléon III furniture, French bronzes, Victorian chairs, various vases and bibelots; all these diverse styles were mingled in a skillful and harmonious disorder—what Boileau called "the harmonious disorder only art can create"—and the paintings of different schools permitted unlimited

**Château de Ferrières**

Left, top: The Salon Rouge is the first reception room of the main floor's enfilade. A tall coromandel lacquer screen and a bearskin rug add exoticism.

Left, bottom: A circle of seating, all originally made for this room during the Second Empire, is gathered around the fireplace in the Salon Blanc.

combinations. The unusual atmosphere of the hall was certainly due to the startling contrast between its stately proportions and the intimacy of its decor, which gave an impression of warmth.

Growing up, Guy and his siblings spent October through December at the château, and he recounts childhood tales of roller-skating in the cellars and riding a small train, which transported food from the kitchen that was separated 150 yards from the house by an underground tunnel. In 1940, the Germans would occupy Ferrières for the second time. Guy, who inherited the property in 1949, upon the death of his father, Baron Édouard, recalls:

> After its requisition by the German Army and the looting of its art collections (only the Boucher tapestries hadn't taken the train to Germany; covered with neatly tacked-on jute-cloth, they'd escaped the notice of the Germans, who hadn't thought of looking underneath

**Château de Ferrières**
Guests gather at a 1959 reception in the Salon Rouge, also called the Salon des Boucher after the tapestries hanging on the walls, and the Salon Bleu beyond.

it)—after the war, in other words, the château remained unfurnished and unheated. . . . A house that is abandoned for twenty years gradually deteriorates . . . and Ferrières had reached the stage of meriting the name given to it by a former employee of my parents who didn't seem to have appreciated the quiet charms of country life: "the château of slow death."[11]

The restoration of Ferrières was a wedding present to Guy's second wife, Marie-Hélène. The completion of the two-year project was celebrated, in 1959, with a ball appropriately themed "Sleeping Beauty"—nearly one hundred years before this celebration, the house was inaugurated with a similarly grand fête. Many of Lami's original sketches still existed, which Samuel studied closely. There were three guiding principles: to emphasize the château's original Renaissance style as interpreted by the Second Empire; to amplify the color with the textiles and carpets playing an important role; and in the large spaces, to create intimate seating groups. Original textiles were used or rewoven and existing boiseries and ceiling decoration were restored. In the Salon Bleu, the nineteenth-century seating was reupholstered in Napoléon III document fabrics—Chinese black silk embroidered with butterflies and flowers, damasks, patchwork, and more. Samuel unified the disparate types of seating by keeping the ground color

**Château de Ferrières**

Above and opposite: Eugène Lami conceived the Salon Blanc, considered the *grand salon*, in the neo-Grec style whose revival was made fashionable in the nineteenth century by the Empress Eugénie. Lami also painted the ceiling decoration of frolicking nymphs in the style of François Boucher. Many features of the room are nineteenth-century reproductions of eighteenth-century examples, such as the Blue Turquin mantelpiece incorporating ormolu fauns after one at the Château de Bagatelle.

of silk and velvet upholstery the same. Each room was centered on some version of a circular sofa or ottoman. To lighten up the dining room, the large chimneypiece was removed to provide increased wall space so that a series of rare hangings depicting the Old Testament tale of the triumph of David over Goliath, which previously hung in the Salon Bleu, could enliven the room with more color.[12]

Baronne Marie-Hélène explained her selection of Samuel: "I really think he was the only choice I could have made to get that particular Napoléon III atmosphere. He's very, very good with everything to do with the nineteenth century, which is of course what made him so ideal for Ferrières. Everything was very well executed and very refined. And I can tell you it's not easy to get the proportions and colors right in a place the scale of Ferrières."[13] Of his own efforts, Samuel modestly said, "All I did was fix things up."[14] Society decorators Jacques and Henri Barroux were commissioned to decorate the bedrooms, and the Danish architect Mogens Tvede oversaw the gardens. After throwing many extravagant balls at the château, the couple decided to donate it to the nation in 1975 in hope that it would have a splendid new chapter.

While Ferrières would become perhaps Samuel's most celebrated and career-making project, he already had been working with several members of the Rothschild family on their historic properties for some time. In fact, he first worked with Baron Guy and his first wife, Alix, at their Normandy property in Reux. Originally owned by Guy's aunt Béatrice, it had fallen into decline after her death in 1934. When Guy and Alix returned from New York after the war, they set about restoring a cottage on the property followed by the château with Samuel's help. Unlike the other Rothschild baronnes, Alix only cared that the furniture was comfortable—she once said, "I have lost too many things to care about possessions."[15] Instead, her great passion was collecting contemporary and modern art, amassing over two thousand works, including paintings and sculpture. She was a champion of young artists, including the painter Balthus. Along with a group of other benefactors spearheaded by collector Vicomte Charles de Noailles, she helped finance Balthus's move to the Château de Chassy in 1953.[16] One wonders about the influence Alix de Rothschild may have had on Samuel's own nascent interest in contemporary art as well as if she played any part in Samuel's barter with Balthus of furnishings in exchange for a painting at this time. Guy continued to work with Samuel after his remarriage in 1957 to Marie-Hélène at Ferrières as well as at their new *hôtel particulier* on the rue de Courcelles, which famously had once belonged to Princesse

Samuel worked closely with several Rothschild baronnes. Opposite: Baronne Marie-Hélène de Rothschild poses for *Vogue* in her rue de Courcelles residence, decorated by Samuel around 1957.

Above, top: From left to right, Baronnes Mary, Marie-Hélène, and Liliane de Rothschild in conversation, 1967. Above, bottom: Baron Guy de Rothschild's first wife Alix, seated, was a noted collector and patron of contemporary art. She is seen here with another Samuel client, Baronne Alain de Gunzburg, and the artist Raymond Rodel.

**23, avenue de Marigny**

A 1963 rendering of the dining room
in the palatial house of Alain de
Rothschild and his wife, Mary. The
couple shared the Paris residence with
Alain's brother Élie and his wife, Liliane,
following the Second World War.
A portrait of Mary by Balthus hangs
over a large console table.

**23, avenue de Marigny**

Above: For Baron Alain's bedroom, Samuel designed an ultra-deep version of a Louis XIV–style sofa, which functioned as a bed.

Right: Another view of the dining room, which was used as a sitting room when not set up for a large dinner.

Mathilde. Here Samuel bestowed the Paris residence with "lots of bronze, glittering and at the same time with plenty of chic."[17]

When the Germans occupied Paris in 1940, the entire Rothschild family had already departed France. Baron Guy was the exception. After being demobilized from the French army and then forced by the Vichy government to sell the family's assets, Guy, with Alix, finally joined his parents in New York in 1941. His cousins Alain and Élie were both captured as prisoners of war, and their childhood home at 23, avenue Marigny, was occupied by the Luftwaffe. This immense *hôtel particulier* was actually two houses joined together with a new facade by architect Alfred-Philibert Aldrophe and expanded in the 1870s by Alain and Élie's grandfather Baron Gustave de Rothschild. The interior decoration began in 1876 and, in true Rothschild fashion, incorporated salons with eighteenth-century French boiseries with a heavier Renaissance style employed in the gallery. Baron

**23, avenue de Marigny**

The grand Salon Rouge epitomizes *le goût Rothschild*, with its mix of magnificent eighteenth-century furniture and works of art acquired by generations of the family. A pair of Rembrandt portraits, depicting a young man and his wife, anchor one end of the salon. The paintings were bought by Gustave de Rothschild in 1877 and are now shared by the Rijksmuseum and the Louvre.

**23, avenue de Marigny**

Samuel provided Baronne Alain with
an elegant and comfortable bedroom
in the Louis XVI style. A television,
framed photographs, and stacks of
books reveal modern life within
the period room.

**Château Lafite**

Baronne Élie consulted with Samuel on the restoration of the storied vineyard's manor house following the Second World War. In the library, often referred to as the Salon Vert after the deep green damask lining the walls, family and guests gather after dinner.

Gustave took no less than Versailles as inspiration for the dining room, whose marble walls were modeled after the salons of Peace and War.

In 1911, Alain and Élie's father, Baron Robert, inherited the mansion and soon decided to make fashionable modifications in the Art Deco style to the private apartments that included a stylish round boudoir for his wife, Nelly, and an avant-garde garden designed by Jean-Charles Moreux complete with a Giorgio de Chirico fresco. Maison Jansen later updated some of the reception rooms in the streamlined neoclassical aesthetic of the 1930s.

Following the war, Baronne Mary and Baronne Liliane, wives of Alain and Élie respectively, both worked with Henri, maintaining close ties with the designer until his death in 1996. Mary focused on restoring the house at 23, avenue Marigny, while Liliane focused on the family's Château Lafite. Alain and Mary made number 23 their main residence, sharing it until 1955 with Élie and Liliane, who at that time moved to the eighteenth-century Hôtel de Masseran. Baron and Baronne Alain restored the main reception rooms but changed the Art Deco style of the private apartments. Just as at Ferrières, Samuel's decoration harmonized with the original eclectic classicism of the existing architecture and sumptuous furnishings. In 1975, 23, avenue Marigny was sold to the nation and currently serves as a guesthouse for visiting heads of state. The couple built a smaller house on the sprawling property, which Baronne Mary de Rothschild trusted only Samuel to decorate. "Where clothes are concerned, the only person I trust is Balenciaga," she quipped. "The same goes for Henri Samuel in the field of decoration."[18]

After the Occupation, the Rothschilds were fortunate to have much of their collections returned to them.[19] In 1946, a group of paintings rescued from the last German-bound train loaded with looted art was the first restitution made to Baron Robert, who died later that year. Other artworks from the Rothschild collections had been sent to Montauban, a storage depot for the national museums, where they were under the careful eye of the Louvre's curators who scraped off the Rothschild labels from the cases. Additionally, many other pieces had remained hidden in the Rothschild properties by the family's loyal employees.

Baron Élie recalled:

> My wife often went by bicycle to avenue Rapp where Carl Dreyfus [from the Art Retrieval Commission] was, with the house catalogue to

find the objects which belonged to us. She was sometimes accompanied by people who worked for us, particularly those who worked in the house who had the possibility of better recalling the objects in question because they had dusted them for so many years. She told me one day that for a piece of furniture she didn't have a photo of, an old butler certified that it had belonged to us. "But how can you prove it," asked Carl Dreyfus. The butler responded, "I am going to prove it to you. If the Germans haven't emptied it out, in the left drawer there will be an old yellow chiffon with which I polished the clock." We opened the drawer and found the yellow chiffon.[20]

Baron Élie was tasked with reviving the family's cherished vineyard and estate Château Lafite, with his wife in charge of the château's refurbishment. Long associated with one of the most celebrated Bordeaux wines, the early-eighteenth-century property was acquired at auction in 1868 by Baron James, who died just three months after purchasing the property. His widow, Baronne Betty, immediately arrayed it in the latest Napoléon III fashion, lavishing it with yards of silk damask from Lyons, furniture from Ferrières, and newly made sofas, poufs, and curtains. Baronne Liliane remininsced about the manor house's condition immediately following the war:

> At the liberation, my sister-in-law Diane and I were the first to return to the château. It had been occupied by the German Army and was in a state of total dilapidation. However, we found to our surprise that the occupiers had installed running water and electricity, whereas before the place had functioned on paraffin lamps and jugs of water. And we were deeply touched to discover that Madame Gaby Faux, who had been left in charge of the estate, had not only managed to conceal much of the books and furniture but had walled up many valuable objects and protected the famous private cellar. All the most important things had been saved.[21]

At the beginning the house was barren. "I remember that when my brother-in-law Alain and his wife, Mary, paid their first visit here our main dish usually consisted of frogs caught on the estate, washed down with a few choice bottles," Liliane noted. The baronne began by pinning surviving scraps of fabric to the walls, followed by commissioning the Lyons silk makers to weave brocades, damasks, and borders following the originals. Family pictures that had been stored in the cellars of the Rothschild bank's Paris headquarters on the rue Lafitte were thoughtfully hung throughout.

**Château Lafite**

Above and opposite: An otherwise simple guest bedroom is decorated with a lively orange-and-blue print in the early 1960s. A pair of twin beds flanks the room's only window.

Liliane's intention in the restoration, with Samuel as her helpmeet, was that all three centuries of the château's life be evident.

Just as at Ferrières, the decoration of each salon is centered on one jewel-tone color. "I think red, green, and blue are the best colors for the pictures and the furniture, and not white walls," Liliane opined in an interview on collecting.[22] "When you see these wonderful impressionist paintings on the white walls of the Musée d'Orsay, you see they've been murdered." Lafite's main reception rooms are the Salon Rouge, which was densely furnished with poufs, settees, banquettes, and *confidantes*—with seating, walls, and curtains in red damask; and the emerald and olive-green Salon Vert, a favorite after-dinner haunt for reflecting on the wines just imbibed. Between the two saturated salons was the palette-cleansing pastel scheme of the dining room: its pale green and pink boiseries were selected to set off the Saxe porcelain service.

However, it was another Rothschild cousin who would prove to be Samuel's most important client. Baron Edmond, also a direct descendent of Baron James, grew up in Switzerland and came to work in Paris at his cousins' bank Rothschild Frères in 1950 at the age of twenty-four, before later open-

ing his own bank. He met Samuel in 1952 at 23, avenue Marigny and soon
employed him to decorate his bachelor quarters, which was just the beginning of their long collaboration.[23]

"Of the three great properties Edmond inherited, Pregny was hands down
the dowager queen,"[24] recalls Baronne Nadine. The Château de Pregny,
situated near Lake Geneva, was built by Baron Adolphe de Rothschild in
1858. Once again architect Joseph Paxton was consulted to design the large
and imposing house and gardens. Baron Adolphe's wife, Julie, referred
to it as "a charming house in the country" and often entertained her dear
friend Sisi, Empress of Austria, there. Paxton also designed a fifty-yard-
long conservatory for Julie's collection of espaliered fruit trees and a
rococo-style aviary for her tropical birds.

In her memoir, *La Baronne rentre à cinq heures* (The baroness will return at
five), Baronne Nadine recounts that when her husband took over the château after the death of his father, Baron Maurice, in 1957, it appeared as a
warehouse, albeit one full of fabulous works of art. "If he had an appreciation for objects, Baron Maurice was evidently not passionate about decoration," she continued. With Samuel's assistance, the boiseries were repainted
and gilded; silk damasks and brocades were rewoven; and a subtle mix
between *le goût Rothschild* and Edmond's personal taste for the eighteenth
century was achieved. "A dream palace emerged," the baronne noted.

Samuel placed many of the pieces Baron Edmond had inherited from his
father and grandfather. In the *petit salon*, there was a magnificent ormolu-
mounted desk by Jean-François Leleu, made for the eminent eighteenth-
century statesman the duc de Choiseul. In the *grand salon*, which featured
large windows that opened out to the gardens, a self-portrait of artist
Élisabeth Vigée-Lebrun was hung with a François Boucher painting of the
Marquise de Pompadour and more lovely ladies by Jean-Marc Nattier. In
the Salon Fragonard, the rococo style prevailed with a spectacular Sèvres

**Château Lafite**

Below: The Louis XIV–period staircase is
one of the oldest parts of the house.

Right: A guest bedroom has shell-pink-
painted boiseries and an alcove for the bed.

porcelain-mounted commode made for Louis XV's mistress Madame du Barry, sympathetically installed among Fragonards and a Watteau. Under the disintegrating silk walls in the library they made the exciting discovery of precious Cordova leather panels. Here they hung a Rembrandt portrait of the artist's wife, Saskia, along with works by El Greco, Bronzino, and Francisco Goya.

"Armainvilliers was where Henri expressed his joy and the depth of his talent," Baronne Nadine states. The Château d'Armainvilliers was a red-brick Anglo-Norman-style pile built at the end of the nineteenth century in a rambling S-form just north of Paris. A huge building, with more than three hundred rooms, it was occupied successively by the Germans and then the Americans in the 1940s. The baronne continues:

> Edmond wished to raze the house and build a smaller one on the lake. I dissuaded him. The house, without being handsome, seduced me. In the *grand salon*, covered in boiseries and hung with a ravishing chintz, we danced the hupa at our wedding.... My father-in-law had installed colored panels, iron shutters and heavy curtains to keep out the light and shrouded his bed in heavy material. The bedroom was furnished with 1925 Art Deco furniture from Czechoslovakia, which was amusing to the point of being ugly. The other rooms had magnificent furniture.[25]

The discovery of Baron Maurice's hunting trophies from India and Africa in the basement of the bank led to the inspiration for the decoration of Armainvilliers, an English hunting lodge belonging to Major Thompson from the late nineteenth century.[26] The trophies, including gazelles, buffalos, zebras, hippopotami, and rhinoceros, were mounted in both the entry and the long gallery, whose walls were covered in dark green fabric and fruitwood paneling. Renaissance furniture from the Paris house of Edmond's grandfather Baron Adolphe was placed in the hall, and Louis XIV–period Boulle-work pieces in the *grand salon*. Edmond didn't wish to use the eighteenth-century paintings he had inherited, and purchased Dutch old-master paintings by artists such as David Teniers the Younger for the house. Samuel had carpets woven that reproduced ancient Persian rugs. In the bedrooms, he had the floral cretonne upholstery made to look faded in order to keep a harmonious, aged appearance. The three-year project was completed in 1963.[27]

With the impending birth of Nadine and Edmond's son Benjamin, Edmond decided to make over the *hôtel particulier* he inherited from his father at 10, rue d'Élysée. Baron Maurice had purchased the property—which had been built for Napoléon III's English mistress—with the intention of transforming it into a museum for his collections. The war interrupted this project and in the early 1960s Edmond gutted the building and hired architect Christian de Galea to build a new house in a "pure eighteenth-century style" with the interiors re-proportioned to fit various boiseries Edmond had inherited.[28]

Inside Samuel was charged with decorating the ground-floor entrance hall and main reception rooms and the upstairs private apartments. In the dining room, he reworked eighteenth-century boiseries from Edmond's

grandfather's dining room by using the embrasures of six old windows as niches in which were displayed four Hubert Robert paintings and a porcelain dinner service. The large Salon Blanc, which opened onto a garden, was furnished with two Savonnerie carpets and eighteenth-century furniture, once belonging to Rothschild cousins, that Edmond purchased at auction. Interior designer Alain Demachy was commissioned to make the basement level into Edmond's private domain, including a gallery to display the baron's Greek and Roman antiquities, a screening room with a vitrine of antique iridescent glass, and a sitting room clad in mother-of-pearl from which a bronze staircase and ramp designed by the sculptor Philippe Anthonioz led to an indoor swimming pool conceived as a tropical lake complete with waterfall and dense plantings of banana trees and ficus.

Rather than installing a particular set of eighteenth-century boiseries inherited from his grandfather, the baron decided to offer them as a gift to the Israel Museum in Jerusalem, where it would be incorporated into the

Baronne Nadine de Rothschild stands in her Paris dining room on the rue d'Élysée, which was decorated by Samuel.

museum's first period room. He recounted, "This dazzling salon, which I don't remember having passed through more than twice in my childhood, slept in a shed, disassembled for twenty-five years."

The Louis XV boiseries were the foundation on which the rest of the room was built. They were originally made in the 1740s for the 46, rue du Bac *hôtel particulier* of Jacques-Samuel Bernard, the son of a prominent banker. After the house was torn down during Haussmann's modernization of Paris sometime after 1876, Edmond's grandfather installed them in his Faubourg Saint-Honoré house, the Hôtel de Pontalba (now the residence of the United States Ambassador to France).[29]

André Malraux approved the export license for the boiseries to leave France, and the museum built a special pavilion to house the room. Samuel then began the two-year project of the room's installation, joined by his favorite lighting specialist, René Klotz. Curator Karl Katz recalls:

Samuel came to Israel with a large team of French artisans. It was precision work at every step. Even laying the hardwood flooring was a daunting task: artisans had to create a special matrix before they could put down the complex marquetry pattern. Samuel took the finest sand he could find, sifted it three or four times until it was absolutely free of foreign objects, and dried it thoroughly in an oven. Then, he laid it on the floor, and his craftsmen slowly tapped the immaculate sand down until it formed a thick, smooth, clean, level, moisture-free, absolutely perfect layer. On such a solidly packed surface, there could be no shifting or warping, and the possibility of moisture seeping in was nil. Atop it he finally laid down the precious wooden pieces.

Slowly, the stupendous room took shape: wooden walls, carved with gilt and white, were tapped into place. Above each of its four doors we reinstalled the paintings of allegorical depictions of Europe, Asia, Africa, and America. Two Gobelin tapestries made for Louis XV flanked the mantel, while mirrors, furniture, sculptures, and candelabras glimmered, just as they had two and a half centuries earlier. Long months turned into years while they slowly reassembled the room, as it had originally stood on rue du Bac in Paris.[30]

On June 24, 1969, the room opened with great fanfare with a large group of celebrants flying in for the occasion. Of the project, Samuel said, "I was able to do it thanks to the admirable boiseries.... The current Baron Edmond added furniture, tapestries, objets, the chimney garniture, paintings, and a superb sculpture by [Guillaume] Coustou destined for this room. The occasion was dreamed to re-create an overall eighteenth-century ambience, which an Israeli visitor today could imagine a grand mid-eighteenth-century French residence." Samuel was under no illusion about the purity of his museum installations. "Even in a Louis XV salon where every element is perfectly authentic, you're forced to finally install electric lights."[31] Samuel helped install a few more period rooms at the museum and would serve as the president of the French Friends of the Israel Museum for several years.

There are many reasons why Samuel was the perfect choice to interpret *le goût Rothschild* for the twentieth century. He hailed from a similar international Jewish banking background and understood the lifestyle of his clients. His association with Jansen and Alavoine, two full-service houses of decoration, had a pedigree of furnishing palaces. But perhaps Samuel's secret to success lays in his own words: "A decor must not be perceived. When you enter a house, it should seem to have always been that way."[32] He made Rothschild opulence look effortless and eternal.

**Rothschild Room, Israel Museum**

The Rothschild Room, opened in 1969, is a celebratory evocation of the French rococo. Period furnishings, such as a suite of giltwood seat furniture covered in Beauvais tapestry, were selected to complement the eighteenth-century boiseries, which were originally made for Jacques-Samuel Bernard and later inherited by Baron Edmond de Rothschild. It was one of the last projects Samuel completed for Alavoine before starting his own firm.

# IV:
# THE MIX MASTER

*I'd be bored living all in the eighteenth century.*
*I'm a twentieth-century eclectic.*

—HENRI SAMUEL

**Henri Samuel, 83, quai d'Orsay**
Samuel's Paris living room arranged
for a 1962 *L'Oeil* magazine article
on contemporary carpets. This
one is designed by the artist Arthur
Aeschbacher, a close friend of
the decorator.

**PLEXIGLAS AND ORMOLU, NEON AND VELVET—**Henri Samuel mixed
the contemporary with the classical to thrilling effect. Throughout his
career, the decorator proclaimed there was no "Samuel style," but that each
project evolved from the client's taste. For himself, he explored bold and
uncommon pairings of new and old and by the late 1950s, clear signs of
a focused interest in contemporary art and design were established in his
residences. Samuel said of his own taste: "Contrary to a certain reputation
I have, I wasn't at all dedicated to the eighteenth-century styles. In those
days, it was simply very much in fashion. People who visit me at home are
sometimes quite surprised at the space I give to contemporary art."[1]

Samuel was always adamant that he didn't collect: "I am not a collector in
the sense of one who systematically buys a type of porcelain or silver to put
in vitrines. I have a horror of vitrines. I love to buy without any methodol-
ogy: a terra-cotta sculpture, an Empire clock, a Rodin bronze, a drawing
by Wifredo Lam, a mother-of-pearl pagoda or a painting by Tal Coat, a
sculpture of Theimer or a painting of Fautrier.... And then everything
gets placed little by little."[2]

114

One of Samuel's first noteworthy acquisitions was *Le fruit d'or* (The golden fruit) painted by the artist Balthus in 1956. When in the early 1950s Samuel first met Balthus, born Balthasar Klossowski, the artist was quickly gaining acclaim for his dreamlike neoclassical style. He created a mythology around himself, including an invented aristocratic past, which took on a physical dimension when, in 1953, he moved into the Château de Chassy in Burgundy. "There was no electricity or running water, though we had the well in the courtyard. The rooms were empty, the sun and rain came in through the roof, and the only heat came from fireplace," remembered Balthus's step-niece Frédérique Tison.[3]

In exchange for a painting, Samuel supplied the artist with furnishings for the almost barren and romantically decaying château, including a sofa covered in a deep gold cut velvet along with matching curtains. Samuel's illustrious clientele greatly appealed to Balthus's sense of grandeur, explicitly referring to Samuel in his memoirs as Edmond de Rothschild's decorator. Samuel specified the bartered picture's size and colors (green in particular because Samuel admired Balthus's handling of the color).[4] The result relates to Balthus's *Les trois soeurs* (The three sisters) series with the new sofa at the center of the composition.

In 1961, while serving as France's minister of culture, André Malraux appointed Balthus as director of the French Academy in Rome, which is housed in the sixteenth-century Villa Medici. Balthus embarked on a restoration of the villa that stripped the rooms to their bare essence. "Restor-

Opposite: Balthus wrote about the restoration of the Villa Medici, the French Academy in Rome, in his memoir: "Everything had faded. It was not abandoned but worn out, colored by time that would have erased it all. I took up the challenge with Roman artisans who had a spontaneous grasp of the old art of gesso."

Above: Balthus and his niece Frédérique Tison at the Château de Chassy in Montreuillon, France, sitting on furniture supplied by Samuel, 1956.

**Henri Samuel, 83, quai d'Orsay**

Opposite: A molded plastic wallcovering in
Samuel's fumoir, circa 1963, provides
a contemporary backdrop for a work by
Pierre Alechinsky and a collection of
primitive objects.

Above: The bedroom, enlivened by a purple-
and-yellow striped satin, reflects the severe
elegance of Louis XVI neoclassicism.

ing the Villa Medici's splendor was a real obsession for me. . . .
Removing the Villa's cheap finery and vulgar furnishings that had
victimized it over the years was a job of rebirth, a form of elevation,"
recalled the artist.[5]

He turned to Samuel again for another sofa—this time in the Knole style
(so called after the seventeenth-century sofa at the eponymous stately
home in Sevenoaks, England, whose elevated sides dropped down to
better function as a bed). This later sofa featured prominently in the
final *Les trois soeurs* paintings of 1963–64. In exchange, Samuel received
the 1961 oil painting *Le panier de cerises* (The basket of cherries).

A 1959 photograph of Samuel's apartment at 83, quai d'Orsay il-
lustrates *Le fruit d'or* hanging over the fireplace in a place of honor.
Samuel selected the colors of the salon to harmonize with the picture:
puce silk for the walls and green velvet for the pair of chaises longues.
Another significant commission was a large painting of the zodiac by
Spanish artist Francisco Bores, from 1956, that was mounted on the

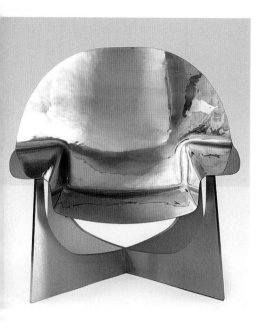

Above: Fauteuil Coque by Philippe Hiquily. Samuel acquired his first pair of chairs of this design, with Plexiglas bases, by 1974 for his quai d'Orsay apartment.

**Henri Samuel, 118, rue du Faubourg Saint-Honoré**

Opposite: Samuel commissioned a brass and petrified wood table (foreground) by Philippe Hiquily in the mid 1960s; it was one of the first pieces of furniture he ever commissioned from an artist. Behind the sofa is François Arnal's Élice console table in Plexiglas.

dining room ceiling. Like many of the pieces Samuel would commission over time, it remained part of the decor for decades.

It is interesting to contrast Samuel's contemporary acquisitions and commissions with the storied collections of his clients. Samuel once told a client that it was because he didn't have the money to buy the best of the eighteenth century as his clients did.[6] Funds may have been one reason, but his friendship with the young Swiss-born artist Arthur Aeschbacher proved to be a pivotal influence in stoking his interest in contemporary art and design. Introduced by mutual friends in the mid-1950s, Samuel soon found himself accompanying Aeschbacher to his artist friends' exhibitions and parties and making the rounds of such contemporary galleries as Alexander Iolas, Marion Meyer, and Dina Vierny, among others. Aeschbacher recounts, "Every year I was invited to an evening with all the surrealist artists—Max Ernst, Dorothea Tanning, Man Ray. All the artists who counted were there."[7] They also attended the late-night parties at the rue du Douanier studio of the sculptor Henri Laurens, presided over by Laurens's mistress Nadine Effront. Reflective of how social circles overlapped, Aeschbacher had been schoolmates with Ninette Lyon, Nadine's daughter, and Nadine herself was the former mistress of the surrealist artist Oscar Dominguez, who turned up at the studio with his current lover, the collector Marie-Laure de Noailles. "At these evenings, there were quite a few Belgians like Magritte. I was dazzled. Philippe Hiquily and I were the young ones at those réveillons."[8]

Vicomtesse Marie-Laure de Noailles and Samuel crossed paths often during the 1950s and 1960s. Aeschbacher recounts a dinner at Samuel's house in Montfort l'Amaury when she brought Dominguez. By the end of the evening, the artist's mischievous antics devolved into his stripping naked. Samuel was not amused. "It was everything Henri detested, as he wanted everything to be perfect," reminisced Aeschbacher. Maintaining proper manners at all times was essential in Samuel's universe.

Aeschbacher introduced Samuel to Philippe Hiquily, but it was Marie-Laure de Noailles who first asked the sculptor to apply his talent to furniture. In 1964, de Noailles commissioned Hiquily to make a table incorporating a slab of porphyry she had acquired on her travels. Its organic form and handworked metal appealed to Samuel, who commissioned the same design, but with a top of petrified wood, for himself the following year. Samuel followed up with a second commission for a biomorphic gueridon, for which he designed the base and that he would eventually order in

Opposite: Samuel commissioned this Diego Giacometti bronze table incorporating caryatids in 1976. It was the first time the artist employed the motif, and it was only at Samuel's insistence.

Right: Diego Giacometti created this staircase for the Switzerland residence of Samuel's client George Embiricos.

multiples. Many more orders for various pieces by Hiquily for himself and clients—including the actress Jacqueline Delubac, department store heir Bobby Haas, Louise de Vilmorin, André Malraux, and various Rothschilds—followed.

According to Aeschbacher, part of Samuel's intention in commissioning these pieces was to support young and often struggling artists. Aeschbacher himself created artwork at his friend's behest for the guest bedrooms of the Hôtel de Paris in Monaco. The result of Samuel's collaborations with these artists was much more than creating a piece for a project: Samuel provided the encouragement and means for the artists to experiment with different forms and materials, often making a significant impact on the artist's course of direction. Gallerist Yves Gastou reflects, "The strength of Henri Samuel was that he dared to include the works of unknown artists and designers in his interiors." Decorative arts historian Yvonne Brunhammer

**Henri Samuel, 83, quai d'Orsay**
Above: Artist Guy de Rougemont's 1970 Nuage table sits prominently in the salon, 1974.

Opposite: A neon sculpture by Ron Ferri illuminates the deep blue dining room. On the ceiling is a mural of the zodiac by Francisco Bores, commissioned by Samuel in 1956. The painting would later be installed in the green library of his Faubourg Saint-Honoré apartment.

further expounds, "He acted as a true patron, like [French fashion designer and art collector] Jacques Doucet, but more generous, as well as more respectful of the talents from which he was able, with his famous tact, to bring out unexpected forms."[9]

During the mid-1960s, Samuel also began commissioning furniture in bronze from the sculptor Diego Giacometti. Until Samuel's last days, most projects included a Giacometti table. The sculptor first applied his skills to the decorative arts for the interior designer Jean-Michel Frank. Between 1929 and 1940, Diego and his brother Alberto created vases, andirons, and most notably lamps and sconces out of plaster, the white hue of which aligned with Frank's spare aesthetic. Unlike Alberto, Diego remained in Paris during the Occupation during which time he mastered the art of bronze casting. Uneven and complex surfaces were his signature and secret, later earning him the moniker "the king of patinas," given to him by a bronze caster. His first pieces of furniture were display stands for his

brother's work, but it wasn't until 1951 that he designed furniture explicitly for a domestic setting. These works were for Swiss patrons and later gallerists Marguerite and Aimé Maeght for their Paris apartment on the avenue Foch and country house in Provence. Samuel's commissions from Giacometti were most often tables and bookcases, and frequently incorporated finely cast small animals, such as birds or frogs. One of the most ambitious projects Giacometti completed for Samuel was a staircase in Switzerland for longtime client George Embiricos.[10]

"Diego, who went to neither museums nor gallery exhibitions, hit upon antique, eternal forms by instinct, conferring on them a new nobility," wrote Daniel Marchesseau in his 1987 Diego Giacometti monograph.[11] The furniture's timeless aesthetic made it pair beautifully with all periods. Samuel kept a small reserve of Giacometti tables, so that even after the artist's death in 1984, he was still able to supply them to clients. One piece he never sold was a square center table embellished with caryatids. The caryatids, not part of Giacometti's usual repertory, were a special request by Samuel and one the artist and client battled over. From its creation in 1976, it held an important place in the designer's famed Pompeian-red salon, and in the Christie's sale of the designer's estate thirty years later, it was the highest grossing lot, selling for over $550,000.

By the early 1970s, Samuel had given his quai d'Orsay apartment a makeover. The only elements unchanged were the Empire *Retour d'Égypte*–style fireplace with the prized Balthus above. In the salon, the taffeta curtains were removed to better emphasize the views of the Seine, and a large lavender-gray rug woven with a contemporary trompe-l'oeil geometric motif covered most of the floor. *Architectural Digest* described its visit in 1974: "An elevator opens directly into his apartment. The eye is immediately dazzled by the lustrous sheen of metal: a statue by Hiquily, copper benches by the same artist, bronze ashtrays and cigarette urns by César, a low Lucite table with a metal border by Guy de Rougemont." This table was one of de Rougemont's first pieces of furniture. After seeing the artist's *Sculpture Volume* series exhibited at the Galerie Suzy Langlois in 1969, Samuel asked the artist if he would consider reimagining the sculpture's silhouette as a table. As someone interested in questioning art's boundaries, de Rougemont was game. "I came to furniture because I wanted to bestow a function on the volumes of sculpture, yet forfeit none of their ambiguity; is it function or not function?" The resulting Nuage (Cloud) featured a brass top and a rose-colored Plexiglas base that was lit from within. The first table was created in 1970, and numbered two from an edition of six.[12] Samuel

**Jacqueline Delubac, 83, quai d'Orsay**

Samuel enrobed the *grand salon* in shades of white to emphasize Delubac's extraordinary art collection, which included Georges Braque's 1936 *Femme au Chevalet* over the fireplace. A built-in bookcase provided a display area for bronze sculptures. To the far right sits a gilt-bronze Expansion lamp with polyurethane shade, created by César in 1976.

**Jacqueline Delubac, 83, quai d'Orsay**
In the green dining room, furniture by
Jansen mixes with oil paintings by, from
left to right, Victor Brauner, Raoul Dufy,
and Wifredo Lam.

later commissioned a smaller version for his own study with a palisander-
veneered top. This spurred a prolific period of creating furniture and
lighting in de Rougemont's career.

Jacqueline Delubac, who also lived at 83, quai d'Orsay, was a Samuel client
with adventurous taste. Delubac was the third wife of the dramatist and
director Sacha Guitry, a Gallic Noël Coward who cast her in several of his
plays and films where she personified the sophisticated Parisienne of the
1930s. After their divorce in 1939, Delubac sold off her jewels to focus on
collecting art, favoring less established artists. "I have a good eye. I had
the good fortune to have enough intuition to buy paintings by Poliakoff,
Fautrier, and Dubuffet when they were not very well known. And I am very
glad that I purchased them when everyone was making fun of me," recalled the actress. After working with Stéphane Boudin of Jansen for forty

years, she called Samuel when she moved into the new apartment. Samuel reused much of her existing furniture, including Jansen's expanding Royal dining table, and commissioned several new pieces. A Nuage-style table by de Rougemont and a brass and petrified wood table by Hiquily livened up the otherwise traditional furnishings in the living room. To emphasize the important art collection, Samuel selected ivory upholstery for the salon's walls. A bottle-green silk damask figured with large foliate sprays was used in the dining room where the astonishing Francis Bacon's *Carcass of Meat and Bird of Prey* of 1980 hung among works by other artists.

**Jacqueline Delubac, 83, quai d'Orsay**
After decades of having blue bedrooms, Delubac—with Samuel—chose a light yellow that she found "quite harmonious." Georges Roualt's large oil painting *Sainte Face* was hung so that it was the first and last thing she saw every day.

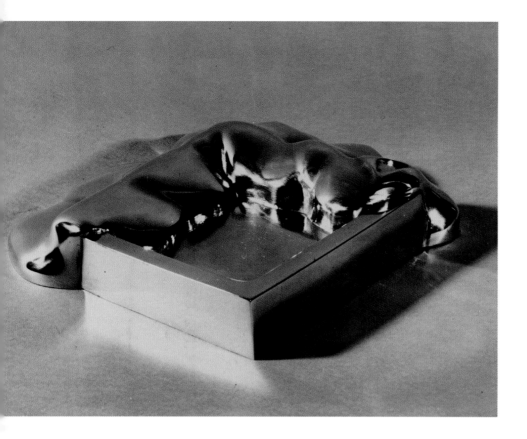

Above: In 1971 Samuel commissioned *Expansion* ashtray in gilt-bronze from César as a limited edition.

**Henri Samuel, 118, rue du Faubourg Saint-Honoré**
Opposite: One entered the apartment via the green velvet entrance-hall-cum-library, which opened on to the Pompeian-red *grand salon*.

Overleaf: Samuel's iconic *grand salon* singularly blended the decorator's love of contemporary art and design with classical high style.

The transparency of acrylic piqued Samuel's interest, as evidenced by the many pieces he commissioned from François Arnal, whom he first met in 1964 and formed a warm friendship with. Arnal, a painter who turned to sculpture in 1960, had the idea for L'Atelier A in 1968: "In 1968, the museums were closed, and 'art is dead' was written on the walls. After this chaos, I wanted to do something else. There had to be a different way to bring young people towards art."[13] L'Atelier A, an experimental collective of artists that operated between 1969 and 1975, believed this could be achieved by artists creating functional and useful items. Art critic Pierre Restany wrote the manifesto:

> Painters, sculptors, young architects are not equipped today to produce the useful and beautiful forms that transform the everyday setting of our lives. Their creative power is therefore condemned to exercise in the solitude of the studio and in the abstraction of an isolated poetic pursuit. Atelier A specifically wants to give these creators a chance, to provide them with the opportunity to produce prototypes of forms, to participate in industrial design or decoration programs, to develop shows or audiovisual environments.[14]

Samuel embraced these useful works of art, never losing sight that they were artistic creations. A Hiquily table or chair was also sculpture in his eyes and he treated it as such by having the piece stand alone in the center of the room where it could be viewed from different angles. The distinc-

tion between furniture-sculpture and his other furnishings was part of his success in mixing and was founded on the belief that the best talents of each era can be combined and make the whole exceed the sum of its parts.

By 1976, Samuel was installed in the apartment where he would live for the next twenty years. Client Nadine de Rothschild had discovered the ground-floor apartment located within the eighteenth-century *hôtel particulier* at 118, rue du Faubourg Saint-Honoré, belonging to Countess d'Harcourt.[15] It comprised a suite of rooms, including his professional office, arranged around a large interior courtyard. Visitors were greeted by Samuel's immaculate majordomo and unrestrained dachsunds and ushered into the forest-green velvet entrance hall-cum-library. A sculptural terra-cotta fountain by the Second Empire sculptor Jean-Baptiste Carpeaux dramatically stood out against the lustrous walls and richly hued mahogany

**Henri Samuel, 118, rue du Faubourg Saint-Honoré**

Opposite: Artist Arthur Aeschbacher created a series of oil paintings scaled to fit the dining room's boiseries. One hangs above a console table by Marco de Gueltzl.

Above: An earlier iteration of the dining room, circa 1978, with a glass-and-Plexiglas table and a pair of Philippe Hiquily pedestals.

Empire furniture. The room's doors were so convincingly painted to look like mahogany that his master *ébéniste*, David Linker, was fooled. Samuel's first Giacometti table seamlessly blended in with the period furnishings.

The *grand salon* was deserving of its name with soaring sixteen-foot-high ceilings and a series of four double French doors opening to the garden along one side. The room was paneled in nineteenth-century boiseries that apparently displeased Samuel but, because the apartment was rented, he was not able to remove. Instead, he disguised them by hanging the walls with Pompeian-red silk noil fabric. In the earliest photographs of the room, published in 1976, one can discern the overdoor panels wrapped

**Henri Samuel, 118, rue du Faubourg Saint-Honoré**

Opposite: Sylvain Dubuisson's 1991 parchment-veneered desk, installed in Samuel's office, was one of the last pieces the designer commissioned.

Above: Across the courtyard were Samuel's private quarters, composed of his bedroom and this small sitting room hung with a Braquenié cotton printed in colors selected by Samuel.

**Henri Samuel, 118, rue du Faubourg Saint-Honoré**

Previous spread: A cozy, old-fashioned ambiance presides over Samuel's bedroom with Georges Le Manach's Plumettes used for the walls and curtains. Just as at his bedroom in the country, chinoiserie touches, such as the black japanned furniture, abound.

in the same silk. (It is unclear if the overdoors that are visible in the 1980s photos were ones replaced to his and his landlady's liking or if he came to accept them.) To conceal the doors' exaggerated proportions, he placed custom screens in the same material in front of them. These screens, on which he hung framed drawings, gave movement and volume to the space without interrupting its unity.

Almost all of his contemporary and modern works of art and design were gathered here. (By contrast, the other more private rooms in the apartment were decorated more traditionally.) To further showcase them, he reduced the room's color scheme to red-orange, black (for the tinted floor, sofas, and curtains), and white (the Cogolin carpet, boiseries, and ceiling). A bold terra-cotta was selected not because he particularly loved the color on its own merits, but because it enhanced the art. Gold was the unofficial fourth color, echoed in ormolu, gilding, and brass touches throughout.

One end of the room was anchored by Balthus's *Le fruit d'or*. To build on the wall's star power, Samuel commissioned from the artist César, whom Samuel had met through Aeschbacher, a bronze console table to sit under the painting. Its organic form, suggesting molten lava, was a characteristic of the artist's Expansion series. In the mid-1960s, César began working with liquid polyurethane, a plastic resin that, upon contact with air, expands in volume and instantly hardens. The result was used to form a mold for the bronze casting. While the artist had previously made smaller items for Samuel, such as ashtrays and cigarette holders in small editions, this console table was the first piece of bronze furniture he ever created (and would remain one of very few ever realized).

The following year Élie de Rothschild commissioned a pair of Expansion andirons from César. The question of how exactly these commissions came about remains unanswered. Samuel used his residences as showrooms and as venues for his frequent entertaining; most of his clients came from his social circle. The documentation doesn't exist to know whether Baron Élie was so impressed with Samuel's console that he took it upon himself to make a direct commission or if Samuel took a more active, official role. What we can surmise is that Rothschilds, Goulandrises, and others most often first saw these artists' works *chez* Samuel before ordering pieces themselves.

Samuel's taste and eye changed with the times and in the late 1980s and early 1990s he commissioned several pieces in anticipation of moving to a new residence where everything was to be modern. From the artist Marco de Gueltzl, he ordered tables and *torchères* made of sand-blasted glass and steel that Brunhammer compared to African jewelry.[16]

One of the last pieces Samuel commissioned for himself was a desk by the architect-designer Sylvain Dubuisson completed in 1992. Executed in luxurious parchment-veneer, its refinement is in keeping with Samuel's aesthetic. Dubuisson recalls:

> I was received in a large room full of objects and furniture that reflected the personality of Henri: open, erudite, generous! Henri was affable, attentive, and at the same time direct. He ordered a version of Office 89, a model that was already in limited production (less than ten were made). But the original size of 180 or 190 centimeters did not suit him because he found it too big for the space he had designated for it. He ordered it in 160. The finishes that were offered—mahogany, oak, or pear—did not suit him either. He asked for his model in parchment! I had never worked in, or thought of using, parchment, which for me was a material of the past, and I was at that time looking toward innovation.
>
> The original model of Office 89 had a space for paper or accessories, which was accessible by rotating a drawer out from under the leather top. [Samuel] didn't want that either, because it didn't seem practical to him, and instead asked for a small classic pullout drawer. The last change he requested was for gray leather. I was charmed by his way of taking over the design in a direction I would never have naturally taken. He opened me up to a less dogmatic world, one that allowed me to collaborate with patrons, men of the world, in a sensitive and generous way.[17]

In his eighty-sixth year, Samuel continued to look to the future. The Dubuisson desk is now in the collection of the Musée des arts décoratifs, bequeathed after Samuel's death by his cousin Michel David-Weill and Michel's wife, Hélène. As one of the last examples of Samuel's enthusiasm for the contemporary and his championing of new talent, it is a fitting expression of his legacy.

Les Rothschild
bâtisseurs et mécènes

AUTHENTIC DECOR
THE DOMESTIC INTERIOR
1620-1920
PETER THORNTON

# V:
# HENRI SAMUEL DÉCORATEUR

*I hate it when people say, "Do as you wish." I like to build on my clients' taste and ideas. The fact is that however refined or inventive a project may be, it remains lifeless if its occupants don't bring to it their own finds or quirks.*

—HENRI SAMUEL

**Count and Countess Hubert d'Ornano, quai d'Orsay**

The *grand salon* has been embellished by decades of the d'Ornanos' collecting, ever since Samuel first decorated the Paris apartment in the mid-1970s.

**IN 1970 HENRI SAMUEL** began a new chapter in his career: Henri Samuel Décorateur.[1] After nearly twenty-five years as the head of Alavoine, Samuel opened his own firm, prompted not by ambition or a desire to have his name at the forefront, but because Alavoine had finally closed its doors. At sixty-six, the designer was internationally acclaimed as a master of French decoration, and both kings of countries and industry clamored for his time.[2]

Samuel set up office on the ground floor of his apartment building at 83, quai d'Orsay, and maintained a small staff to oversee all projects. In addition to Madame Chaminade, his secretary, and Jacqueline Lallemand, his accountant, Jacques Cayron, and a Monsieur Hanché were his design associates along with a full-time draughtsman. When Samuel moved to

**Robert Zellinger de Balkany, Hôtel de Feuquières**

Above and opposite: For the private rooms of Balkany's Paris house, Samuel effected a cozy version of *le goût Rothschild*. In the sitting room, Braquenié's Le Grand Corail print provides a dynamic background to de Balkany's collections of bronze and ormolu works.

118, rue Faubourg Saint-Honoré, around 1976, the staff worked out of a small office in his apartment where a miniscule stairwell led to a drawing studio above. "Pierre, a tiny man who drew incredibly in the style of Louis XV, Louis XVI, Empire, drafted the plans for everyone," recalled the architect Christian Magot-Cuvrû, who began working with Samuel in the early 1980s.[3] Work was intense, but the office was run with civility. Every day Samuel would take lunch at Maxim's or Le Relais at the Plaza Athénée, often dining with friends such as the Duchess of Windsor. "Teatime at Monsieur Samuel's was very important. Around 4:30 p.m., his majordomo would come to serve us tea and it was this moment of pleasant relaxation when we spoke of everything and nothing for thirty minutes," remembers Magot-Cuvrû.

In addition to his office, Samuel established his own upholstery workshop located at 39, Cité Industrielle, near the Bastille, overseen by Daniel Delaplace. Delaplace succeeded his father, Lucien, in 1978, who in turn had been running the atelier since 1946. In the mid-1970s, David Linker, a master *ébéniste* at the exclusive Cour de Varenne workshop, was hired to work for Samuel exclusively.

**Robert Zellinger de Balkany,
Hôtel de Feuquières**

In the study, Empire mahogany
furniture and cerise-striped silk strike a
masculine note.

Working with such a prominent clientele called for absolute discretion. Linker recalls that at the Cour de Varenne, one had to be invited to purchase the important eighteenth-century furniture that passed through the workshop, and it was understood that should the buyer want to resell, he would do it through the Cour de Varenne. In this way, important, often royal, pieces could be tracked and their restoration never compromised. When Linker or his colleagues helped deliver a piece to a residence, they were never told the owner's identity.[4]

Samuel patronized the same artisans repeatedly so that they essentially became an extension of his team and knew his preferences intimately. Atelier Mériguet-Carrère began collaborating with Samuel while he was still at Alavoine around 1965, and provided the painting, including faux finishes, for all his projects. The firm prided itself on delivering a high level of service to its demanding clientele. Antoine Courtois, who has worked at

Mériguet-Carrère since 1991, recalls the designer's preference for clear, light colors based on eighteenth-century precedents. Courtois elaborates:

> His decorative schemes had the *boiserie* painted in three monochrome shades on bases of white or gray, the fields always receiving the most sustained tones, the panels in medium tones and the moldings remaining the clearest and brightest. Another specific feature of the Mériguet-Carrère workshop is that it is very important that painted decorations were made with water, never oil, because, inevitably, they turn yellow in time. The glazes and decors thus retain the correctness and freshness of the original choice of Monsieur Samuel. A little detail: In every project, Samuel placed a faux ivory shagreen wastebasket made by the Mériguet-Carrère workshop.[5]

Samuel was very specific about color and was always on site to supervise

**Robert Zellinger de Balkany, Hôtel de Feuquières**

Red velvet and ormolu add opulence to the master bedroom, which includes a mahogany-paneled bathtub. Over the fireplace hangs a Felix Kelly painting of the Château de Sainte-Mesme, de Balkany's property in Yvelines.

Château de S.te Mesme. A. Serebriako.

**Robert Zellinger de Balkany, Château de Sainte-Mesme**

The Salon Bleu is furnished more rustically than the rest of the residence, with hunting trophies and provincial antiques in keeping with the manor house's fourteenth-century origins.

the custom mixing of colors, which could take hours to get to his satisfaction. This clear vision and uncompromising insistence on perfection extended to all elements of a decor. Laurence du Plessix, who worked in Samuel's office from 1984 to 1987, remembers Samuel's dissatisfaction with a carpet that was too bright, resulting in the decorator adding dust to make it visually more subdued. If a molding wasn't exactly what he wanted, Samuel would have it remade, even at his own expense.[6]

After the restoration of the Château de Ferrières and his work at Versailles, Samuel was firmly established as a master of the historical interior as well as one of the most adept interpreters of *le goût Rothschild*. Shopping center magnate and polo enthusiast Robert Zellinger de Balkany was one client who was attracted to the latter style, desiring a suitably grand backdrop

## Robert Zellinger de Balkany, Château de Sainte-Mesme

Right: Brilliant reds and blues animate the Louis XIII–style dining room that seats twenty-four.

Below: De Balkany's admiration of Carlos de Beistegui's taste is on display in the library, which features a spiral staircase similar to those in de Beistegui's own library at the Château de Groussay.

151

**Robert Zellinger de Balkany, Château de Sainte-Mesme**

In the small dining room, Samuel fancifully mixes English Regency furniture with Braquenié's Le Grand Genois tree-of-life cotton print.

for his wide-ranging collections, which included English and Italian old-master paintings and seventeenth- and eighteen-century ormolu-laden furniture of royal provenance. For the Hôtel de Feuquières, his Paris residence at 62, rue de Varenne, Balkany commissioned Samuel to decorate the second floor,[7] which included his bedroom and study along with a small sitting room. While these were not the grand reception rooms, they were the rooms most often used by the client, and indicate that Samuel was known to provide comfort as much as style.[8] Wall-to-wall carpeting and upholstered walls formed a cozy cocoon. For Balkany's bedroom and study, severe Empire furnishings lent an imperial note, appropriate for the tycoon whose tastes veered toward the grandiose. At Balkany's twelfth-century Château de Sainte-Mesme in Yvelines, a less magnificent style pervaded. Unmistakable references to Carlos de Beistegui, the wealthy South American collector-decorator much admired by Balkany, abound; in the library, a mahogany spiral staircase evokes those at Beistegui's Château de Groussay.

Samuel revisited Ferrières's Second Empire opulence for Hubert and Isabelle d'Ornano. In the mid-1970s, when the young couple, with their five children, first found the apartment in a building on the quai d'Orsay erected in the 1920s, it was an empty gray box with exposed lightbulbs but distinguished by ultra-high ceilings and large windows overlooking the Seine. The couple asked Samuel to evoke old-world Poland, a nod to Isabelle d'Ornano's noble Radziwill ancestry. At the time of its completion in 1976, designer François Catroux enthused, "You feel like you are sailing through some Polish river, the Vistula perhaps, and discovering fabulous things like forests on its banks. There is much more to it than specially copied Oriental carpets and printed material on walls. It is not a contrived decor."[9]

The acquisition of a set of Louis XV doors from Versailles, painted in imi-

tation green marble picked out in gold, inspired the main salon's scheme, and coordinating boiseries were installed. The countess knew she wanted a painted ceiling: "The idea came to me when I was crossing some corridors at the Vatican!" She also specified no curtains, "Just shades, because the view is so lovely. And I rarely lower those, as the Seine is so alive at night with the lights on the boats. Since there are no curtains, I wanted the fantasy to be in the carpet."[10] Samuel designed striped taffeta silk Austrian shades—unlined to let the light atmospherically filter in. A fitted Braquenié carpet inspired by an ancestral rug belonging to the countess's family covers the entire first floor, unifying the entrance gallery, salon, dining room, and master bedroom. In response to the clients' request for a tented dining room, a false domed ceiling was created, with both ceiling and walls hung in a Braquenié *indienne* cotton print. The family's collection of Polish paintings was clustered here. The countess noted, "I arranged the room as a dining room as well as a living room because having a real dining room is such a loss of space."

The d'Ornanos, owners of the skincare and cosmetics company Sisley Paris, entertained frequently and the contiguous entrance gallery, salon, dining room, and master bedroom were designed to be opened as a circuit during receptions. An elliptical mezzanine was installed in the bedroom and provided, beyond visual drama, an upper dressing room. Samuel used much of the furniture from the clients' previous apartment, which had been decorated by Jansen. Here, as with projects for many of his clients, the designer was highly adaptable and willing to work with existing furnishings and collections.

As the d'Ornano children grew up, the couple turned to collecting contemporary art, adding a new twenty-first-century layer to the original Proustian mise-en-scène. "I love establishing a dialogue with an artist that gives birth to a work of art. And then that work of art becomes integrated

**Count and Countess Hubert d'Ornano, quai d'Orsay**

Opposite: In the dining room, paintings and family photographs, some pinned to the two small draughts screens, are clustered around a red velvet sofa.

Right: Samuel designed the domed dining room ceiling to give the effect of a tented room. Cherished reminders of the past are everywhere: nineteenth-century Polish paintings hang on the wall and a collection of family silver is on display in a black lacquered vitrine.

into our everyday life, nurtures our life, becoming something with which we live. We want our home to be welcoming and our door always open to the unexpected," the countess observed.[11] Samuel considered this project an extremely successful and happy collaboration between client and designer. He appreciated that the d'Ornanos had such strong tastes and ideas. Just as with Jean-Michel Frank's iconic parchment-sheathed salon for Marie-Laure and Charles de Noailles, the decoration for the d'Ornanos has become even more alluring with the clients' personal additions over the years.[12]

At the Château Margaux, Samuel explored his penchant for the severe classicism of the *first* Empire, a taste acquired from his mentor Stéphane Boudin. When the Ginestet family, who owned "the Versailles of the Medoc"[13] since 1934, were compelled to sell, it was deemed such an important French property that its sale to an American buyer was blocked by the

government. Greek entrepreneur André Mentzelopoulos, who was already well established personally and professionally in the country, was approved to purchase the celebrated but struggling vineyard in 1977. After André's death in 1980, his wife, Laure, took over, quickly earning respect from the wine community for her improvements to the property and the vineyard's output. These efforts included the restoration of the stately Palladian-style château itself. Although built in 1810 to the pure neoclassical designs of architect Louis Combes, the existing interior decoration was a Napoléon III pastiche. Mrs. Mentzelopoulos turned to Samuel, with further advice from Jean Feray, the chief inspector of Historical Monuments.

Mrs. Mentzelopoulos with Samuel's support decided to interpret the rooms in the original 1810 Empire style of the building. Samuel reflected, "It was necessary above all to avoid the wish to reconstitute a style that had never existed as such at Margaux."[14] Without the need to adhere to an aca-

**Laure Mentzelopoulos,**
**Château Margaux**

Opposite: Samuel selected a rosy terracotta color not only to add warmth to the entrance hall's severe neoclassicism but also to stand in relief to its imposing architectural elements.

Above: To keep the *grand salon* from becoming too formal, Samuel purposefully had the moldings of the boiseries picked out in white, not gold.

demic refurnishing plan like at the Grand Trianon, the designer sought to
bring to the château the charm of the style without the pompousness, with
fresh colors and a bold mixing of patterns. On the main floor, the large
entrance hall led to an enfilade of reception rooms, including a salon,
library, and dining room. Samuel described the restoration: "The doors,
the cornices, the chimney pieces, and the mirrors were intact, and we even
found quite a few pictures in the château, mostly in the very large staircase. The large entrance hall was an off-white color, so I had it repainted
a color I call Pompeian, which is brighter than terra cotta; and I redid the
floor in black and white marble, the way it originally was."[15] The rose-
hued walls dramatically set off the room's architecture. Combes had designed the hall's two niches to receive statues of Achilles. Samuel and Mrs.
Mentzelopoulos found Roman emperors to stand in for the Greek war-
rior. The designer continued, "I completely changed the dining room—it
had been done in Napoléon III furniture and there was black flocked
paper on the walls, which I repainted and marbleized, making them extremely light."[16] The walls were further embellished with a painted frieze
of grapevines. On the upper bedroom floors, Samuel diverged from the
restrained classicism below with chinoiserie decoration.

Samuel recalled, "There was very little furniture in the château, and
what there was was very simple, so we used some of that in the guest
rooms. Then we went out and furnished the entire château as it would
have been, had the interior been completed at the same time as the exterior."[17] An unusual practice in France at the time, Samuel selected antiques
from various dealers and brought them to Margaux on approval. Samuel
and Mrs. Mentzelopoulos sat in two large chairs in front of the house to
examine each piece as it was unloaded off the truck. The client, like a Roman emperor at a gladiator fight, gave a thumbs up or thumbs down before
a piece was placed inside the house or, rejected, sent back to Paris.[18]

A personal passion project came a few years later in the restoration of the Musée Nissim de Camondo. The *hôtel particulier*, built by Count Moïse de Camondo between 1911 and 1914 at 63, rue de Monceau, was modeled loosely after the Petit Trianon in order to showcase its owner's exceptional collection of eighteenth-century fine and decorative arts. Each painting and piece of furniture was carefully selected for a specific place. The Camondo family, sometimes called "the Rothschilds of the East," were Jews of Spanish descent who had made a banking fortune in Constantinople immigrating to France in around 1869. Moïse de Camondo had intended for the house and its contents—a reflection of a lifetime of collecting—to go to his son, Nissim, but after his son's death during aerial combat in the First World War, he gifted it to the nation. Moïse de Camondo lived alone in the house with a staff of twenty until his death in 1935. The Camondo family would know further tragedy when its last remaining members, Moïse's daughter and grandchildren, perished at Auschwitz a decade later.

In 1984, the Union des arts décoratifs created the "Pour Camondo" committee, with the eminent antiques dealer Didier Aaron as president, to

**Musée Nissim de Camondo,
63, rue de Monceau**

Opposite and above: Samuel joined the Paris museum's restoration committee in 1986 and immediately underwrote the restoration of the entrance hall so that visitors would have a positive first impression. He would often use a postcard of the entrance's staircase when sending notes to friends.

**Musée Nissim de Camondo,
63, rue de Monceau**

Right: The oak-paneled library expresses the ambience of *l'art de vivre* that the restoration committee cited as a guiding principle to their efforts. Samuel shared with the committee his thoughts on successfully lighting and re-creating upholstery and draperies for a period room.

Overleaf: Count Moïse de Camondo's bedroom was one of the last rooms to be restored. Samuel's own workshop was responsible for the new curtains and seat upholstery.

An elevation of Antenor Patiño's *grand salon* in his 38, avenue Foch duplex apartment, illustrating the installation of a pair of important early-eighteenth-century chinoiserie tapestries. The drawing was prepared in 1981 by architect Christian Magot-Cuvrû, who was assisting Samuel on the project.

revitalize the mostly forgotten museum. At Aaron's invitation, Samuel joined the committee as vice president in 1986. Like Aaron and Samuel, many committee members and donors shared the Camondos' Jewish heritage, and restoring the museum took on an additional dimension. While Samuel never identified as a religiously devout Jew, he once said that his heart was Jewish—and in his eighties lent financial support to this museum and various organizations in Israel. Samuel was a champion fundraiser, rallying many clients to become benefactors including Edmond de Rothschild, Nancy and Frank Richardson, Susan and John Gutfreund, and Jerry Perenchio as well as soliciting a large donation from the top Paris antiquaries. Samuel himself underwrote the restoration of the entrance hall and grand staircase. Samuel selected the entrance as he believed it was vital to make the first impression as inviting and distinguished to visitors as possible.

Moïse de Camondo had stipulated that nothing, down to the framed photographs on his bedside table, could be moved or changed during the house's life as a museum. Samuel commented on its importance: "It's the perfect ensemble of eighteenth-century decorative arts. Everything is in its place because it was a home. It's just absolutely first-class."[19] The restoration, done room by room, included cleaning boiseries, tapestries, and paintings; reweaving curtains and upholstery, in some instances by the original Lyonnaise fabric producers; and restoring the paintings, furniture, and objects. The Mériguet-Carrère workshop was entrusted with restoring the boiseries, including cleaning, regilding, and painting, as well as cleaning the ormolu mounts on the furniture. Samuel's own upholstery workshop made the curtains for several of the rooms. Samuel stated, "The surroundings are as authentic as it was possible to make them: old woodwork, panels, overdoors, mirror frames and cornices recovered from old houses, were carefully installed at the beginning of this century in rooms rebuilt to fit them." Samuel's strong interest in lighting the rooms in a sympathetic,

organic way helped animate the house museum. In 1990, Samuel led First
Lady Barbara Bush on a tour, when all but two bedrooms had been completed. "We want to start all over again," she exclaimed when it was time
to depart. In 1987, Samuel was made a chevalier of the Legion of Honor
for his contributions to the nation's culture, of which the Musée Nissim de
Camondo was just one.[20]

Samuel's last client was the Roman fashion designer Valentino Garavani,
who in 1995 acquired the Château de Wideville, a seventeenth-century
residence built by a finance minister to Louis XIII just outside of Paris. The property is stately, but, only one room deep, maintains a sense
of intimacy. Just as he had selected the quintessentially English firm of
Colefax and Fowler to decorate his London house, the couturier wanted
the top French designer for Wideville. "I wanted to make it as perfectly
French as the château itself and Samuel was the best decorator in France. I
loved working with him. I wanted to have a fresh approach . . . not gloomy
or too frilly . . . with perfect decoration and great fabrics and colors. And
he is the only one who doesn't want to give a bourgeois look to a château,"
recalled the couturier. "We did every room together. I am quite particular
and love to put my nose everywhere. Even if I admire the decorator, I have
to say my opinion."[21]

Valentino's influence can be seen in the splashes of pageantry—enormously
scaled armoires, flashes of leopard—that animate the rooms. His predilec-
tion for chinoiserie led to the creation of the tour de force winter garden
sitting room. Jack Setton, the previous owner, had hired Renzo Mongiardino to decorated the principal floors. As conceived by Mongiardino,
the winter garden was an office paneled after the Duke of Urbino's Renaissance *studiolo* in elaborately inlaid wood with the groin-vaulted ceilings
frescoed with classical motifs. With the assistance of architect Alain Raynaud, Samuel stripped this decoration away, reinstalling the paneling in an

upstairs room. In its place, arched Chinese paper panels hand-painted with flowering trees, masses of porcelain, and a *famille-verte* palette transformed the dark office into an airy oasis visually in harmony with the verdant formal gardens outside. Of the designer who returned a historic château to its original splendor, Valentino marveled, "He is one of the most modern and fast-thinking decorators I have ever worked with."[22]

**Valentino, Château de Wideville**

Above: At the end of his career, Samuel often referenced schemes from past projects. This assortment of fabric swatches used for Wideville's living room (right) included several Samuel had used in the billiard room for client Jerry Perenchio a few years earlier.

# VI:

# F.F.F.

*I hardly brush my teeth without asking Henri first.* —JAYNE WRIGHTSMAN

Samuel often looked to the severe elegance of the Empire style for his design of entrance halls, as illustrated here for clients Nancy and Frank Richardson at 820 Fifth Avenue in the mid-1980s.

**IN POSTWAR AMERICA,** the "Louis Louis" look became *de rigueur* among a certain high-society set. Art historian Bernard Berenson mused in his diary, "Their paradise is a period piece of the eighteenth-century French, where every object is supposed to have been used by historical personages of the French court. As if French people of the Versailles period were always living as the super-wealthy Americans in their leisure are decorated by their interior decorators to live."[1] By 1962, the fashion for French design was so pronounced that interior designer Billy Baldwin dubbed it F.F.F. (an abbreviation for "Fine French Furniture").[2] This craze brought a branch of the quintessentially French restaurant Maxim's to Chicago in December 1963, whose opening included a Dior fashion show. To faithfully reproduce the historic Belle Époque interiors, the owners sought out Henri Samuel.[3]

Samuel was working steadily in the United States by the 1960s. Jayne Wrightsman, one of New York's most distinguished enthusiasts of F.F.F., began working with Samuel following the retirement of her longstanding decorator Stéphane Boudin of Jansen. Samuel's collaboration on the Wrightsman Galleries at the Metropolitan Museum of Art heralded his undeniable position as one of the world's most eminent interior designers.

By the time Henri Samuel and Jayne and Charles Wrightsman began working together in about 1966, the couple had already cemented their reputation as discerning connoisseurs and collectors. After securing his fortune,

**Jayne and Charles Wrightsman,
513 North County Road**

Opposite: After the death of the Wrightsmans' longtime decorator Stéphane Boudin
in 1967, the couple turned to Samuel who
applied a less formal hand to the interiors
of their Palm Beach residence. He painted
the entrance hall a cheerful salmon pink
and encouraged Jayne Wrightsman's
enthusiasm for Anglo-Indian ivory furniture.

Above: In the reception room, Samuel
whimsically installed a window and framed
the ocean view with a gilt surround to
surreal effect.

Oklahoma oil tycoon Charles Wrightsman set his cap at conquering
the upper echelons of high society, and it was his second wife, Jayne
Larkin, who would help achieve this nurtured goal. A few years after
marrying, they purchased in 1947, complete with contents, Blythe-
dunes, a six-acre property at 513 North County Road on the coast of
Palm Beach. Built in 1917 and remodeled in 1931 by local architect
Maurice Fatio, the two-story stucco and red-tile-roofed house belonged
to the stylish Mona and Harrison Williams, whose decorator, Syrie
Maugham, had created a blanc-de-blanc scheme, with the exception
of the living room's dazzling aquamarine-blue Chinese wallpaper that
showcased Mona's famous blue eyes. By acquiring the celebrated taste-
makers' house with its interiors intact, the Wrightsmans were buying
an instantaneously chic backdrop. Charles soon began playing Pygma-
lion to his young wife from modest origins, equipping her with tutors
in French and art history and a wardrobe by Mainbocher.

**Jayne and Charles Wrightsman,
513 North County Road**

In the library, a large ivory goatskin rug
adds a surprising contemporary note.

**Jayne and Charles Wrightsman,
513 North County Road**

The dining room's Louis XV boiseries
set the design direction for the room.
Four of the twelve dining chairs,
reupholstered by Denning and
Fourcade, are pulled up to the table.
Three panels of a seventeenth-century
Chinese screen are positioned in front
of a door; its other half was installed in
the Wrightsmans' London apartment.

Just as style setter and international best-dressed Mona Williams was a
model of emulation for Jayne, so was automobile heiress Thelma Chrysler
Foy, who, upon her death in 1957, was hailed by the *New York Times* as "the
woman of the greatest taste in the current life in New York."[4] Foy began
collecting French furniture in the 1940s and is widely credited with introducing a Francophile taste to the smart set. Jayne's first collection—Meissen
porcelain birds—was inspired by the one Foy herself had formed.

However, it was the Baroness Renée de Becker, whose mother was a grand-
daughter of the Grand Baron James de Rothschild, who educated Jayne
on the finer points of F.F.F. At the outbreak of the Second World War,
de Becker came to New York and by 1949, she had established herself at
820 Fifth Avenue in a grand floor-through apartment centered around a
forty-foot entrance gallery that led to a circuit of large reception rooms.

**Jayne and Charles Wrightsman,
513 North County Road**
Jayne Wrightsman's gray and aqua
bedroom is full of books, reflecting
the connoisseur's deep interest in the
history of fine and decorative arts.

With the help of Jansen, it was transformed with boiseries and parquet de Versailles floors into a temple of French eighteenth-century refinement. Ailsa Mellon Bruce exclaimed, "The salon of Baroness de Becker was like heaven to us. She taught us the possibilities of wealth. She taught us how to live."[5] Mellon Bruce, Wrightsman, and others could purchase a piece of the baroness's universe by buying one of her antiques from the dealers Rosenberg and Stiebel, who acted as her brokers. In 1956, when de Becker decided to return to Europe, the Wrightsmans purchased her apartment, which, like the Harrisons' house before, already bore the imprimatur of established taste. The baroness's decorator, Stéphane Boudin, who had already been given carte blanche with the Wrightsmans' house at 513 North County Road, continued to work closely with the couple. The Palm Beach house became a receptacle for all the eighteenth-century treasures the couple began seriously acquiring by 1952. Jayne noted:

> [The house] must have been hideous at the time, but I wasn't aware of it. We were having too good of a time. Boudin was so adorable. We both loved him. He made a laugh out of everything. It was so amusing to do things with him, we never wanted to stop. He found everything for us— the furniture, the boiseries, the porcelain, the parquets. He did all the curtains and all the covers—everything. Little by little the house began to fill up in the early '50s, and in 1955 we bought the apartment in New York. So of course we cleared out vast amounts of the best things from Palm Beach, and then we began filling up the house again.[6]

Indeed, some did find the high-style interiors a bit overblown for the resort town, but the Wrightsmans' generous hospitality, attended to by an indoor staff of twenty, attracted many, including neighbors Senator John Kennedy and his young wife, Jacqueline. "To stay at North County Road was an unforgettable experience, a tangible reminder of the *douceur de vivre*, the passing of which was lamented by Talleyrand. The company, the life, the service, presided over by Domenico, the gardens, the swimming, the conversation and not least the cuisine were all incomparable," noted one visitor.[7] Cachepots were filled with roses grown on the property that bloomed continuously for years at a time, and houseguests found their favorite flowers waiting for them in their rooms, a special touch copied from Mona Williams.

Impressed by Judge Irwin Untermyer's relationship with the Metropolitan Museum of Art's curators stemming from the promised gift of his English decorative arts collection, the Wrightsmans began to forge their own association with the institution. In 1958, the museum's director James Rorimer arranged for the art historian Francis Watson, who compiled the Wallace Collection's magisterial catalogue of furniture, to do the same for the Wrightsmans. The resulting five volumes were published by the Metropolitan Museum in 1965. As the Wrightsmans accelerated their purchasing, by one account spending $16 million through the 1960s, pieces would first go to Palm Beach before coming to the Metropolitan.[8] The star of the collection—a red lacquered *bureau plat* made for Louis XV by *ébéniste* Gilles Joubert in 1759—was purchased by the Wrightsmans in 1969 for $350,000. Watson hailed it "the most important piece of French furniture in America."[9] The Wrightsmans positioned it in their Palm Beach drawing room until 1973, when it became the centerpiece of the Varengeville Room at the museum.

Throughout the Palm Beach house, "we had a great deal of coral velvet and fringes, and we tried to cover everything as exactly as it would have been in the eighteenth century. Not until much later did we pull it all off and put cottons there instead," recalled Jayne. "When Stéphane Boudin became too ill to continue, we began to work with Henri Samuel, another Parisian, who also became a close friend."[10] In a 2000 interview with Jansen historian James Archer Abbott, Jayne compared Samuel to his first mentor, Boudin: "Henri Samuel and Stéphane Boudin were exactly the same. They were talented in the same ways . . . [they both had a] great interest in detail while concerned with the whole composition and its success."[11] However, Samuel brought a more relaxed approach to the decoration more in keeping with the tropical locale. Jayne noted, "The house here took on a lighter look, became less pompous. Henri Samuel bought much simpler things, changed the carpets, painted the entrance hall salmon pink, and redid the reception room. And I started buying all that crazy ivory furniture."[12]

Swapping out woven silks for printed cottons, Savonnerie carpets for white bisque fur skin rugs, and gilt wood for ivory were a few ways the designer played down the formality. Perhaps his most profound touch of simplicity was found in the reception room. He installed a large window over the sofa and framed the resulting view of two palm trees with a thin gilt surround so it appeared to be a painting.

In 1982, the Wrightsmans hired Vincent Fourcade of the firm Denning and Fourcade to refresh the rooms with new upholstery. After Denning and Fourcade completed only a few rooms, including the large salon,

**Jayne and Charles Wrightsman, 513 North County Road**

The glorious *grand salon* is an amalgamation of the decorating talents of Syrie Maugham, Stéphane Boudin, Henri Samuel, and Vincent Fourcade.

Charles, reputedly chagrined by either the great cost or the length of time it was taking, decided to sell the house in 1984.

Undoubtedly one of the Wrightsmans' attractions to working with Samuel after Stéphane Boudin's retirement was his experience working with curator Gérald Van der Kemp at Versailles. Ever since 1963, when the couple provided the funds for the Metropolitan Museum of Art to acquire the 1730s boiseries from the Hôtel de Varengeville and the Palais Paar, their primary focus was planning for the opening of the French period rooms that would bear their name.

Historian Bruno Pons, who has written extensively about the history of French boiseries, describes the American "French period rooms" as "plausible installations, carried out with the historical knowledge of the time regarding the furnishings of French 18th century homes, and dependent upon the objects owned by the museum. The intention was no longer to re-create, but to evoke."[13] The first gallery of French period rooms at the

Metropolitan Museum of Art, comprising five interiors, opened in 1954. In November 1969, when the Wrightsman Galleries were unveiled, the Varengeville Room and the Paar Room were the new additions gifted by Jayne and Charles, along with a modified Morgan Alcove, named after financier J. P. Morgan, who had donated the alcove's boiseries years before. Until 1966, Stéphane Boudin was heavily involved, even discovering the Palais Paar boiseries that found their way to the museum via Philip Sassoon's English country house. For the Varengeville Room, Jansen's workshop created nine new panels to enlarge and augment the boiseries. These rooms were furnished mainly with loans of important objects from the Wrightsmans with the aim "to exhibit in a tasteful manner outstanding examples of the interior architecture and decorative arts of a period." Samuel recalled:

> I was already working for the Wrightsmans, who asked me to install the rooms they had gifted to the Metropolitan. The idea was to remake all the rooms of furniture and decorative arts around old boiseries which had once been in French châteaux or *hôtels particuliers* in a spirit very different from that of the Louvre. It was to evoke an era by reconstructing a decor, that is to say in achieving all the details, like the curtains, in the spirit of the period. You know, we are in a museum and not in a house and I am without any illusions on the authenticity of the rooms reconstructed. The boiseries, to begin with, have a story: they were for the most part remounted many times during the nineteenth century. Cut down or repainted, it was necessary to give them color. And in so doing there are errors of interpretation that can be committed! On the other hand, during the eighteenth century, one arranged rooms differently. They didn't have this one placement that they have today and far from being placed definitively like in the Second Empire, were placed against the walls and moved according to need. For the receptions, the domestics carried the chairs. Furniture was … movable and changed from one house to another, according to the displacements. Perhaps, only in little rooms like the boudoir of the Hôtel Crillon at the Metropolitan, can one best suggest a period.[14]

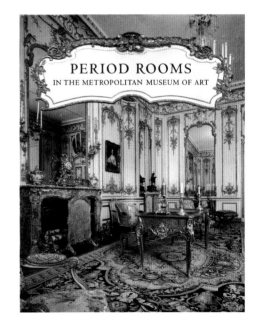

The Metropolitan Museum of Art's 1964 guide to their period rooms features the Varengeville Room on its cover. The red lacquered desk, hailed as the most important piece of French furniture in America, and the large carpet were both in the Wrightsmans' Palm Beach *grand salon* before their installation at the museum.

The 1970s brought more refinements to the galleries under Samuel's guidance, with ceiling heights increased and lighting—always critical to the decorator—made subtler. In May of 1970, Charles wrote to the museum: "I have employed Alavoine for the Museum to see if we can straighten out the horrible De Tessé room and the room with the pink walls where the Kress furniture is located. These are two horrors and must be reworked."[15]

**Wrightsman Galleries, Metropolitan Museum of Art**

The boiseries of the Sèvres Room, circa 1977, were painted to complement the museum's collection of Sèvres porcelain-mounted furniture.

Ironically, Alavoine had supplied the De Tessé's Louis XVI period boiseries to Herbert N. Straus in 1931 for his Horace Trumbauer–designed East 71st Street house. Straus died in 1933 before the house was completed and in 1942, his widow donated the paneling for this room as well as the Louis XVI period paneling for what the museum called the Bordeaux Room. Following Charles's direction, the museum dismantled the De Tessé boiseries and shipped them to France, where more panels were made to accommodate the allocated space for the installation. It was decided to repaint them a gray-green color. The room reopened to the public in November 1972, with Louis XVI furnishings placed within.

The following November the Cabris Room opened featuring Louis XVI period boiseries formerly installed in the Wrightsmans' own Fifth Avenue dining room, now enlarged with eight newly made panels. As the *New York Times*

**Wrightsman Galleries,
Metropolitan Museum of Art**
Samuel designed this Louis XIV–period
room in 1987 around a set of tapestries
already in the museum's collection.

reported, Samuel took great pains to address the lighting in all the rooms. He told the paper, "The ceiling was like gruyere cheese. Mon Dieu—those spotlights everywhere!"[16] These were removed and small-scale Wendel-type recessed projectors were installed to cast a soft, romantic light.[17] Additionally indirect lighting, such as the bulbs in the candelabras and illumination concealed behind the rooms' windows, was made brighter.[18]

Between 1976 and 1977, the galleries were remodeled and enlarged, taking on their current configuration. The Sèvres Room, with boiseries from the Hôtel de Lauzun,[19] was added to the galleries. At the turn of the twentieth century, the paneling had been stripped of its original paint, described in 1903 as "all in oak of the finest texture and deliciously mellow tone."[20] To differentiate it from the other rooms' boiseries, "it was decided that the relief carvings of this room should be painted in light, harmonious colors on a pale straw-colored ground (*jaune paille* was the eighteenth-century descriptive term for this shade), and that the carved naturalistic detail, such as flowers and swags of leaves, or sheaves of wheat, should be painted in the colors they possess in Nature," explained curator James Parker.[21] Samuel supervised their painting in Paris in a palette inspired by the watercolors of the eighteenth-century artist Pierre Ranson. Jayne recorded in a letter to Parker: "While in Paris we went out to see the Lauzun boiserie. It is perfectly enchanting and the colors will be marvelous with the Sèvres furniture."[22] Samuel also supervised the manufacture of three large door frames for the Morgan Alcove.

Samuel's final contribution, in 1987, to the Wrightsman Galleries was a Louis XIV bedchamber. Instead of boiseries, a set of four needlework hangings commissioned by Madame de Montespan in 1684–85, already in the museum's collection, directed the room's design. Samuel, assisted by Harold Eberhard Jr., who previously worked for Jansen's New York office, based the architectural details on those at the Hôtel Salé in Paris (now the Musée Picasso). The balustrade set in front of the state bed was modeled after a pair of oak balusters from the Metropolitan's Hoentschel collection. Sumptuous crimson cut velvet dressed the walls.

While roundly heralded as a resounding success when unveiled, in 2007 Jayne and the museum's current curators agreed it was time for an update. White ceilings, dated lighting, and a furniture plan not necessarily coherent or edited were a few of the elements that were addressed.

In June 1984, the Jack and Belle Linsky Collection opened in galleries adjacent to the Wrightsman rooms. Comprised of nearly four hundred works ranging from old-master paintings to Renaissance jewelry, many of the objects were small in scale. The Linskys, manufacturers of office products that included the Swingline stapler, formed the collection over forty years, buying on impulse whatever pleased their eye. After years of being wooed by several museums, Mrs. Linsky finally decided to bequeath the collection to the Metropolitan Museum, with the restriction that it must be shown together in perpetuity. She was so impressed with the presentation of the Wrightsman rooms that she requested Samuel's involvement. The concept for the circuit of eight rooms was that they suggest a collector's home, so that certain spaces were hung with gold damask and had floors laid with parquet de Versailles. Samuel and Eberhard determined the proportions of each space, including ceiling heights that varied from room to room, and designed the architectural moldings, bronze railings, and marble pedestals.

Cutting-edge fiber-optic lighting was incorporated into the display cabinets.[23] The Linsky rooms opened to the public in June 1984.

After the unveiling of the Wrightsman Galleries, Jayne and Charles purchased a London residence. In the summer of 1971, Samuel was at work decorating the couple's duplex apartment at 21 St. James's Place in the heart of Mayfair. While the residence featured an alluring wraparound terrace overlooking Green Park, it was located in a postwar building with low ceilings and few distinguishing architectural details. Always mindful of what is appropriate, Samuel selected wall-to-wall ivory carpeting and upholstered walls rather than the boiseries and parquet floors of their other residences, which could look out of place in these smaller spaces. Some pieces from their Palm Beach residence, such as a set of shell engravings from the entrance hall, eventually found a new home here. The main sitting room's palette of muted green and garnet red was taken from the large nineteenth-century Agra carpet.

Elizabeth (known as Lee) and Lawrence Copley Thaw Sr. were another Francophile couple, albeit with a markedly different collecting philosophy than the Wrightsmans, who trusted Samuel to deliver a classic French backdrop for their F.F.F. "All the Parisian ecstasy over provenance seemed to [my husband] exaggerated. He did not care that the duc de Penthièvre had sat on this chair, or that the princesse de Lamballe had written on that desk," said Lee. The Thaws bought their eleven-room Park Avenue maisonette in the early 1950s and went to Paris to shop because Lawrence had a "total but almost cavalier devotion to all Louis XV and XVI furniture. He felt that the era's gifted craftsmen could do no wrong." For paintings, the Thaws purposely steered clear of the wildly priced Impressionist market and focused on eighteenth-century French and English portraits to round out their collecting. As many of his clients have remarked, a Samuel interior doesn't go out of style. "I'm quite happy with what I have. Unlike dresses, tables and commodes don't need updating. I look at the rhythms of a Jacob chair with continuing delight, just as I find in the music of Mozart an ever-increasing joy," Lee concluded.[24]

One of the great honors of Samuel's career was to oversee the decorations of a state dinner, celebrating America's bicentennial and two hundred years of Franco-American relations. On May 18, 1976, Valéry Giscard d'Estaing, president of France, hosted two hundred guests at the French embassy in Washington, D.C., in honor of United States President Gerald Ford. The concept for the festivities was to bring Versailles grandeur to the back lawn

**Lee and Lawrence Copley Thaw,
Park Avenue**

Left: Among the prized pieces in the
Thaws' New York living room were a
portrait of the Countess de Montchal
by Nicolas de Largillière and the rare
blue-ground Aubusson carpet woven
with a pattern of gardening tools and
ladies' hats.

Above: Lee Thaw, dressed in an
Empire gown in the entrance hall
of the Park Avenue maisonette,
channels the American enthusiasm
for French furniture.

of the embassy where an enormous tent would be purpose-built and decorated. Always meticulous, Samuel traveled from Paris twice to check on the tent's manufacture by the Philadelphia firm Vanderherchen. The two hundred guests were dazzled by the magnificent event. The *Washington Post* reported, "The tent defied recognition as a tent. An estimated 1,200 yards of fabric copied from an Empire period silk, lined the walls. Five large tapestries, borrowed from Versailles, hung at intervals, the spaces in between punctuated with portraits of famous Revolutionary War American and French heroes brought over for the occasion from the Louvre. Red, white and blue embroidered voile cloths, specially made by the French linen firm of Porthault adorned the long tables."[25] Giscard d'Estaing expressed his gratitude to Samuel in his personal inscription on the program: "For Monsieur Henri Samuel, A souvenir of a triumphant evening to which his taste contributed greatly."

In the 1980s, Guy and Marie-Hélène de Rothschild went apartment hunting in New York. When the baronne was asked why she hadn't considered 820 Fifth Avenue, home to the Wrightsmans, Stavros Niarchos, and French banking scion (and Samuel's cousin) Michel David-Weill, she wittily replied that it would have been too much of a *mille-feuille*, after the cream and puff pastry composed of many rich layers stacked on top of each other. When Nancy and Frank Richardson moved into the building's fifth floor, they eschewed the current English chintz craze for one built around collecting in the tradition of the Rothschilds. While the apartment may have appeared to a visitor as a mini-Versailles, Nancy, a distinguished art and antiques expert who wrote for *House & Garden*, notes, "Henri's work may have been high style, but it was never stiff."[26] Creating spaces where people could comfortably convene was essential to Samuel. While working with the decorator, Nancy also learned the importance of paying attention to a space's lighting. Samuel favored gentle pools of light, with the help of strategically placed uplights, to show off people and collections to advantage. Before

**Lee and Lawrence Copley Thaw,
Park Avenue**
Samuel created for Lee Thaw an
Empire bedroom worthy of the
Empress Joséphine, complete with
leopard-patterned carpet.

**Nancy and Frank Richardson, Northwood**

Framed panels from Zuber's Le Paysage à Chasses hang in the Empire-style dining room of the Richardsons' Long Island manse.

decisions were made, each decorative element had to be examined in the room where it was planned to go. If a fabric was intended for curtains, it had to be looked at vertically.[27] In 1989, Samuel continued to work with Nancy at Northwood, her Normandy-style fifty-room country house built in 1948 for John Schiff in Oyster Bay Cove.

The 1980s in New York was a heady time of maximalist extravagance stoked by the roar of Wall Street. When Salomon Brothers CEO John Gutfreund and his wife, Susan, moved from River House to 834 Fifth Avenue in 1987, the residence's Henri Samuel–decorated interiors made a splash. *Women's Wear Daily* reported:

> It's the talk of New York and one of those lucky few who have sneaked a peak at Susan and John Gutfreund's apartment says it is the "most lavish and beautifully opulent" home in the city, a place that truly has the atmosphere of a house and not just a flat. The duplex, formerly Charles Lachman's apartment at 834 Fifth Avenue, is reported to have

**Nancy and Frank Richardson,
Northwood**
The extensive use of a printed
toile makes a visual impact in this
sitting room.

a magnificent, stone-paneled two-story entry hall with a grand staircase
"big enough to ride horses up it" and a Monet painting of water lilies.
No less impressive is the bowling alley–size drawing room, peppered
with fine French, English and Russian 18th and 19th century furniture, the cordovan leather–paneled library with mahogany bookcases
and silk velvet upholstered furniture and a plant-filled room called the
winter garden. The winter garden is decorated in the Chinese style,
with 18th century painted panels and trellises, all reminiscent of Brighton Pavilion.[28]

Susan had been introduced to Samuel by Jayne Wrightsman and soon
became a cherished client and pupil of the decorator. Samuel guided the
Gutfreunds with even the choice of the domicile. He counseled against an
Italianate town house in favor of the twenty-room apartment located on the
seventh and eighth floors of the 1929 Rosario Candela–designed building.
He particularly approved of the large windows that offered spectacular
views, even when sitting, of Central Park. Antiques purchased during the
Gutfreunds' travels in Europe inspired the decoration of the winter garden room, which was flooded by too much natural light to function as the
originally planned library. Susan recalls, "[The scheme of the winter gar-
den] grew from eighteenth-century painted canvas panels, from a Belgian
château. We purchased them years before at the Biennale des antiquaires
in Paris. They were so beautiful. We had no place for them then, but knew
that one day we would use them."[29] Gilt-trelliswork paneling made of resin
gave order and fantasy to the room.

With the assistance of architect Thierry Despont, Samuel knocked out
walls to create a fifty-foot-long living room, laid the floors with parquet
de Versailles, and uncovered windows in the stairwell to let more light in.
Susan remembered, "[Henri] would sit and stand in the room, observ-
ing the color from all angles, in the bright morning light, as well as in the

afternoon. He studied it with lamplight. . . . He always came himself, never sending an assistant. He was like a couturier, always fine-tuning details."[30]

The dining room was furnished with a suite of eighteenth-century white-and-Wedgwood-blue-painted Adam-style furniture from Jayne Wrights-man. Continuing in the English neoclassical vein, Samuel based the rug's pattern on one at Sir John Soane's Museum in London. The curtain design was taken from the eighteenth century, with the pink under-curtain fabric a gift to Susan from Karl Lagerfeld. "Henri gave you the perfect base, like a couture dress that was sheer perfection whether you added jewels or not," his client, now an interior designer in her own right, explains.[31]

The Gutfreunds soon acquired a Paris residence, a wing of the eighteenth-century Hôtel de Bauffremont on the rue de Grenelle whose other wing was occupied by the French couturier Hubert de Givenchy. Architect Alain

**Susan and John Gutfreund,
834 Fifth Avenue**

A suite of eighteenth-century English
furniture, once belonging to Jayne
Wrightsman, continues the dining
room's blue-and-white scheme.
The giltwood dining chairs are in
ticking stripe slipcovers, a device
Samuel enthusiastically recommended
to his clients.

**Susan and John Gutfreund,
834 Fifth Avenue**

Samuel designed the Winter Garden
room around a set of eighteenth-
century hand-painted canvas panels.
Even on gray days, the room maintains
a warm glow with its gilt wall moldings
and domed ceiling painted to resemble
the sky. The Gutfreunds found many of
the room's features themselves,
including the English porcelain mantel.
"A room by Henri Samuel is like a
haute couture little black dress," notes
Susan Gutfreund. "You add the
accessories and make it personal.
But the black dress has to be perfect:
curtains and upholstery perfectly made,
paint perfectly done, boiseries perfectly
installed, so if the room were empty,
you'd see the perfect detailing."

**Susan and John Gutfreund,
Hôtel de Bauffremont**

A small hall, faux-painted by Atelier
Mériguet-Carrère, in the four-story Paris
apartment Samuel decorated for the
Gutfreunds in the late 1980s. The two
marine paintings previously belonged to
fashion designer Hubert de Givenchy,
who lived in the house's other wing.

Raynaud supervised significant architectural refinements including the reinstatement of the rooms' original proportions. Throughout the wing's four floors, period fireplaces and parquet de Versailles were installed. Atelier Mériguet-Carrère[32] painted the grand salon a luminescent pale gray inspired by a color found at the Petit Trianon. Scroll-armed velvet sofas were based on one belonging to Louis XIV's brother Monsieur in the private apartments at Versailles. This was a favorite model of Samuel's, which he used as early as the 1950s at Baron Alain de Rothschild's avenue Marigny residence. A collection of *verre eglomisé* pictures and a magnificent crystal-and-amethyst chandelier added sparkle while simple cotton slipcovers in a ticking stripe brought an informal ease. The room's approachable

**Susan and John Gutfreund,
Hôtel de Bauffremont**

Above: A large trompe-l'oeil painting of a bookshelf, given to the Duke and Duchess of Windsor by Tony Duquette and later acquired by the Gutfreunds, anchors the library's far wall.

Overleaf: The *grand salon*'s elegant simplicity belies the meticulousness Samuel demanded in the carrying out of each detail. Velvet sofas and chairs of his own design were inspired by eighteenth-century examples.

**Susan and John Gutfreund,
Hôtel de Bauffremont**

Above: Samuel designed the romantically draped four-poster bed in the master bedroom.

Opposite: In the pale blue boudoir, a fanciful chandelier, incorporating a bird perched in a cage, previously belonged to style icon Mona Bismarck.

and highly livable elegance encapsulate Samuel's style. On the ground floor, which opened to the courtyard, the Gutfreunds entertained by candlelight in the intimately scaled dining room.

After visiting the Gutfreunds' New York apartment, entertainment mogul Jerry Perenchio decided Samuel was the ideal person to restore the property he had just acquired in Bel Air, a residential enclave in Los Angeles. The house's exterior was famous for its exterior use in the 1960s television show *The Beverly Hillbillies*. Designed by architect Sumner Spaulding for Lynn Atkinson, an engineer who loved the Louis XV style, the limestone-clad reinforced-concrete residence took five years to complete, replete with a 150-foot-tall indoor waterfall and pipe organ. When the house was finished in 1938, Atkinson's wife, Berenice, took one look and asked, "Who would ever live in a house like this?" The residence sat empty until it was sold in 1947 to Arnold Kirkeby, whose family sold the house to Perenchio

in 1986. Over time, Perenchio added three contiguous lots to the estate, which now sprawls over ten acres.

In the introduction to *875 Nîmes: The House and Gardens*, a book privately printed in 1995 by the Perenchios and named after the house's address, Samuel wrote:

> Jerry had just acquired a splendid estate in Bel-Air, and Susan [Gut-freund] suggested I redecorate the house, which had been built in 1935 in the typical French eighteenth century style reminscent of *La Lanterne* in Versailles. As attractive as was the exterior of the house, the interior had to be completely redone. At first I hesitated. Los Angeles is a long way from Paris, where we would find most of what we would need.... Then Margie [Jerry's wife] appeared on the scene, and the three of us agreed in every way as to what the house should be—not

**Margie and A. Jerrold Perenchio, 875 Nîmes Road**

Opposite: Samuel insisted that to successfully create eighteenth-century-style interiors at this Los Angeles residence, the house had to be gutted. In the entrance hall, new glass-paned doors helped flood the previously dark space with light.

Above: At the end of the entrance hall is the *grand salon*. Green-striped silk walls provide a harmonious background for Mr. Perenchio's important art collection, including works by Camille Pissarro and Claude Monet that are placed over a pair of Louis XV commodes.

a museum, but a comfortable home with very fine antique furniture, creating the best environment for the important collection of fine art that Jerry had assembled.[33]

Perenchio agreed to Samuel's demand that everything, down to the roof's slope, must be redone in order to achieve a "proper representation of an eighteenth-century château."[34] Over the next five years, working with architect Pierre Barbe, also an octogenarian Frenchman, the house was gutted, rebuilt, and decorated. Before the building's south facade was rebuilt, a crew of twenty-six painted a full-size trompe-l'oeil version of the elevation for the Perenchios to approve. To source limestone that matched the original, Samuel and the Perenchios flew by helicopter from quarry to quarry in France to find the perfect stone, and then employed a local couple to live on site to ensure that it was quarried properly. Perenchio elaborated:

**Margie and A. Jerrold Perenchio, 875 Nîmes Road**

Samuel had the boiseries of the dining room painted in an eighteenth-century polychrome fashion similar to those in the Sèvres Room in the Wrightsman Galleries at the Metropolitan Museum of Art.

Eleven rooms, including the Morning Room, Library, Dining Room, Garden Room, and Bar, were designed by Henri and built in France, then installed here by over forty French craftsmen. Throughout the ground floor and first floor, they finished the walls [previously travertinc] using *stuc pierre*, the process of applying a mixture of powdered limestone and plaster to create the look of limestone blocks. Under Henri's decoration they painted and finished most of the rooms. I must offer words of praise for the French craftsmen. They were outstanding. They took pride in their work, performed on budget, honored their contracts precisely, and always conducted themselves professionally.[35]

The entrance hall was transformed with a new staircase designed by Barbe and a limestone-and-black-marble floor, which replaced the former green and black marble. The front and interior doors of wood were replaced

**Margie and A. Jerrold Perenchio, 875 Nîmes Road**
Samuel designed the demi-lune plaster overdoors in the oak-paneled library. A Diego Giacometti bronze table sits in front of the sofa.

**Margie and A. Jerrold Perenchio, 875 Nîmes Road**

A printed cotton copied after an eighteenth-century silk covers the Morning Room's walls and windows. The coved plaster ceiling, created in France, had to be cut down to fit into a Boeing 747 for transport; it was reassembled on site.

with glass ones, so that what was once a dark space became a light-filled, welcoming one. The domed plaster ceiling of the Morning Room proved to be one of the most ambitious architectural features. Made in France in one piece, the ceiling was too large to fit through the freight door of a Boeing 747—it had to be cut into sections for transport and reassembled onsite.

In early November of 1991, the Perenchios finally moved in. "It was a wonderful adventure and one of the greatest learning experiences of our lives, as this extraordinary artist taught us and guided us for five years in the realization of our dream," enthused this—one of many—grateful client.[36]

**Margie and A. Jerrold Perenchio,**
**875 Nîmes Road**
Mr. Perenchio considered the living room's sixteenth-century Chinese carpet one of the rarest antiques in the house. The room was used for concerts and film screenings. Audio speakers and sound equipment were concealed behind the Chinese screens.

**Margie and A. Jerrold Perenchio,
875 Nîmes Road**

The Garden Room, located at one
end of the *grand salon*, was designed
around a set of Japanese lacquer and
mother-of-pearl panels that Samuel had
previously owned.

**Margie and A. Jerrold Perenchio,
875 Nîmes Road**

In the new pool house designed by
Pierre Barbe, Samuel employed a
streamlined neoclassical style.
Maple furniture in the Charles X style
is arranged in the faux-limestone-
painted interior. An alcove tented
in striped cotton recalls Napoléon's
Château de Malmaison.

# VII:
# LEGACY

*Fashion changes, but style endures.* —COCO CHANEL

**"I ALWAYS ADMIRED HIS PERFECT TASTE,"** acclaims Hubert de Givenchy, the legendary couturier who had many friends and clients in common with Henri Samuel.[1] Samuel brought this "perfect taste" to his work, expertly and elegantly interpreting historical styles for contemporary living. He was proud that there was no so-called Samuel style, that one couldn't instantly identify his hand in a room. It was more important that the interiors he created reflected his clients' personality and functioned as a life-enhancing backdrop. Samuel had a passion for living well and an interest in contemporary life that infused his work with a sense of both well-being and dynamism. This resulted in the landmark decoration of his Pompeiian-red salon, which has become a highly influential twentieth-century interior. It is considered pioneering for its pairing of classic French high style with contemporary design for an overall effect that continues to surprise and dazzle.

For a designer who delighted in the past but embraced the present, it is fitting that both his classical and contemporary contributions to design are celebrated today. During his career, high-profile commissions for the Rothschild family and the palace of Versailles demonstrated his command of historical styles. One American client with traditional taste admitted that he might not have hired Samuel if he had first seen the decorator's own residence because of the mysterious sculptural furniture by François Arnal, Philippe Hiquily, Ron Ferri, Guy de Rougemont, and other artists populat-

Galerie Yves Gastou has re-editioned several Philippe Hiquily pieces originally made for Samuel. The decorator first commissioned the armchairs and the modular dining table, which can be configured in several ways, for the Paris dining room of client Bobby Haas.

ing his salon. Today, it is via this furniture and how Samuel incorporated it into a high-style decor that a new generation is learning his name for the first time. Yves Gastou, who worked with the sculptor Philippe Hiquily and now with his estate on a new edition of Samuel-edited[2] pieces, states, "All the great decorators and architects are inspired by Henri Samuel. He was an initiator who dared to include little-known artists in his interiors. He had the courage to depart from the ponderous eighteenth- and nineteenth-century styles with a wonderful eclecticism. He was a pioneer."[3]

In November 2014, the New York gallery Demisch Danant opened the exhibition *Paris Match: Henri Samuel and the Artists He Commissioned, 1968-1977*. Gallery co-founder Suzanne Demisch notes, "Henri Samuel captured an environment that still resonates today. He represents a new age, a time of decorators who were successfully mixing historic material with contemporary art and objects in a very glamorous way."[4]

Swiss architect Rodolphe Pierre Lasser worked for Samuel between 1955 and 1960, while simultaneously attending the École Camondo. Lasser recalls:

> This was when Henri Samuel was at the height of his career. He was working all over the world. These years, from when I was twenty to twenty-five, were very important to me and were essential to the future success of my own business. One of Samuel's greatest strengths was his sense of public relations. He was very social and invited everywhere.

Upon arriving in Paris, Lasser presented himself to the *antiquaire* Maurice Chalom, who, impressed by the young man's drawings, referred him to Samuel. During his time at Alavoine, Lasser prepared drawings for several major Samuel projects, including the châteaux de Ferrières and Belleville, and several deluxe hotels: the George V in Paris, the Ritz in Lisbon, and the Hôtel de Paris in Monte-Carlo. Lasser remembers:

> Samuel kept his distance from his employees and was sometimes impatient. It was not always easy to know what he wanted. But in general he was very proper and he greatly appreciated the artisans he worked with.... I loved my years in Paris. I was enriched culturally, but financially it wasn't easy as we weren't well paid—it was difficult to pay for food and my *chambre de bonne* lodging. But it was stimulating.

Lasser returned to Geneva in 1960 and subsequently founded the highly successful Maison R. P. Lasser, which comprised an interior design office

Swiss interior architect Rodolphe Pierre Lasser created this rendering while working for Alavoine in the late 1950s as a possible design treatment for Samuel's own apartment.

and the furniture workshop his master *ébéniste* father had previously established in 1929.[5]

Like Samuel, the interior designer Jacques Grange prides himself on the diverse nature of his work. With an academic understanding of the past, he has the pulse of the present. "I don't want to stay with established taste," Grange has said. "I like to take risks." He has created densely layered interiors for collectors such as Pierre Bergé and Yves Saint Laurent as well as spare, curated ones for others. While working for Samuel between 1965 and 1968, Grange experienced the charge of collaborating with artists, such as Diego Giacometti, and continues to incorporate contemporary creations in his own work. "I was twenty-three, and everything was possible," he recalls. "I wanted to work for Monsieur Samuel—he was like a king—and start decorating immediately. I'd been interested in nothing else since I was fifteen. It was my passion."[6] The world of haute decoration is a small one, and Grange's work has overlapped with Samuel's many times. The next generation of Samuel's clients have turned to Grange, such as beauty entrepreneur Terry and her husband, Jean de Gunzburg, whose parents Baron and Baronne Alain de Gunzburg lived in an *hôtel particulier* decorated by Samuel. Terry de Gunzburg recounted to *Architectural Digest*, "As our mutual friend Pierre Bergé says, 'Jacques has the talent for doing houses that don't look done up,'" a sentiment Samuel would have approved of.[7]

During the 1980s, architect, designer, and artist Thierry Despont assisted Samuel on several of his New York projects. His authoritative understanding of the classic French *ensemble* has drawn historical properties such as the Hôtel Ritz, which he recently renovated, to his door. "There is a natural elegance in well-thought-out French eighteenth-century interiors. It's all about getting the proportions right," notes the architect. "But I want it to be comfortable. It can't be like Versailles, where you don't feel like you can sit down."[8] One of his earliest projects, for which he received much acclaim, was the centennial restoration of the Statue of Liberty in 1986. "That project taught me that you need to learn as much as you can about a structure before you touch it. We spent years drawing it, figuring out how it was built. That structure was absolutely brilliant. You cannot practice architecture without knowing history." Despont's private clientele, like Samuel's, ranks among the world's most affluent. He approaches his residential commissions with the *ensemblier* mentality: "I like to create a small universe. From the master plan to the doorknobs, from the trees planted outside to the way people will sit and eat and dance inside, you create and control a whole microcosm," elaborates Despont.

Opposite: Rodolphe Pierre Lasser brings together an eclectic array of styles in one of the reception rooms of his Geneva office.

Overleaf: Architect Thierry Despont, who worked with Samuel on several New York projects, oversaw the recent restoration of the Hôtel Ritz in Paris, including the Vendôme Suite, conceived as a classic French ensemble.

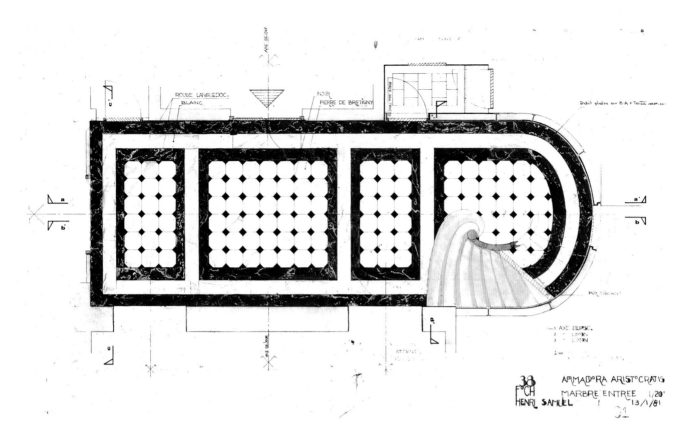

ARMADORA ARISTOCRATIS
MARBRE ENTREE 1/20'
38 FOCH
HENRI SAMUEL 13/1/81

Starting in 1981, architect Christian Magot-Cuvrû worked with Samuel on several projects, beginning with an apartment for Bolivian "King of Tin" Antenor Patiño at 38, avenue Foch. "When I worked with Samuel, I was young and I was truly mesmerized by all the projects we worked on. It was extraordinary, such French elegance! His taste was very classical and extremely elegant. There was a great simplicity in his decors."[9] Magot-Cuvrû collaborated on one of Samuel's last projects, the seventeenth-century Château de Wideville for the couturier Valentino. He continued to work at Wideville after Samuel's death, overseeing the transformation of the estate's historic *pigeonniere* into a chinoiserie fantasy.

Few interior designers have embraced the spirit of the *ancien régime* as fully as Jacques Garcia, who has made the historic Château du Champ de Bataille his home since 1992. For *dix-huitième* enthusiasts the world over, Garcia has achieved almost heroic status. His handling of period style is animated with a theatricality he calls "controlled abundance." Most recently Versailles's curators consulted with Garcia on the refurbishment of the king's apartments, as Gérald Van der Kemp did with Samuel fifty years before. Both designers were commissioned by client Robert Zellinger de Balkany to decorate rooms in his rue de Varenne *hôtel particulier*. Garcia was given the *fumoir*, which he hung in deep green velvet set off by bursts of gilt furniture and framed portraits. If Garcia's work is flamboyant, it shares its first and foremost raison d'être—of creating an atmosphere for its inhabitants to enjoy—with Samuel's. "I'm one of the last repositories, in France, of what is called

Above: Architect Christian Magot-Cuvrû made this rendering of client Antenor Patiño's entrance hall at 38, avenue Foch, while working for Samuel in the 1980s.

Opposite: A richly furnished salon at the seventeenth-century Château du Champ de Bataille, the residence of interior designer Jacques Garcia.

Interior designer Delphine Krakoff is known for her compass-setting eye. In this New York living room, she creates an inviting and cohesive space that showcases important design with wildly varying aesthetics, including pieces by Guy de Rougemont, George Nakashima, and Claude Lalanne.

the grand style. And I intend to do everything in my power to keep the chain from breaking, the spirit from being lost," Garcia says today.[10]

A designer who shares Samuel's enthusiasm for eclecticism is Delphine Krakoff of Pamplemousse Design in New York City. "I remember seeing images in the 1990s, in a Christie's auction catalogue, of Henri Samuel's iconoclastic Paris apartment. It was filled with artwork by Balthus, Atlan, César, and Hiquily, combined with cutting-edge contemporary as well as neoclassical design. I was taken by his unexpected and fearless commitment to a unique vision, his understanding of the history of design and architecture without being constrained by it. History is just a point of departure in his design process."[11] Krakoff's own work plays with strong and surprising juxtapositions. Like Samuel, she often pairs a classically articulated room with experimental pieces, so that it looks like it has been furnished over time. As a collector herself, her interiors reveal a personal taste through the layers of art and sculpture, but, like Samuel's, they are thoughtful and edited. "He influenced my work with the idea that a room can be intricate yet simple at the same time."

Henri Samuel's name is almost unknown by younger generations of American designers. Brian J. McCarthy, who opened his New York office after years of working for the esteemed firm Parish-Hadley, is one exception.

The evolution of Henri has always fascinated me. When I think about his first apartment that was so classically eighteenth century compared to the last home he did for himself, it is clear he was always bringing curiosity and new thinking to his design. He introduced any number of artists and furniture designers that we revere today and his living room was a sort of salon style of the arts in a way that wasn't didactic or obvious. It didn't feel gallery-like.[12]

Like Samuel, McCarthy relishes the opportunity to engage and collabo-

Brian J. McCarthy creates a bespoke environment with architecture and wall decoration that engage in an engrossing pattern play. As McCarthy admired in Samuel's own salon, this living room retains the warmth and comfort of a home while presenting a collection of art and objects in an intriguing way.

rate with artists. "It's been the biggest game changer for me and how I see what I do. We do so many wonderful, unique commissions for people. Introducing something that is one-of-a-kind and not recognizable is one of the details that really makes a room stand out." Essential to Samuel's work were his clients' own collections, which brought an added dimension of personality to the room and also made the resulting decoration a collaboration. McCarthy remarks on how, with the twenty-first-century's pervasive expectation of immediate gratification, the art of collecting is disappearing.

> Today people don't spend the time to find things, and they don't take the time to enjoy the process of finding things. And by finding, and seeing, and looking, and doing all of that, you're learning. And that's the only way one can begin to separate the good from the great.

McCarthy ruminates further on why Samuel's interior decoration still beguiles and surprises today:

> There's an order and structure to classical French rooms and while Henri would bring that order to them, there'd be something that would shake it and break it, and make it youthful. There's something so smart about the way he decorated; it's beyond timeless. If you re-created one of Henri's rooms, it would look as fresh today as it did then. To me, that speaks volumes about how great he was. He was a genius, pure and simple. He should be an inspiration to all.

# ACKNOWLEDGMENTS

ATTEMPTING TO DO JUSTICE to the epic career of Henri Samuel was a daunting task, and it would not have been possible without the support of so many. Gratitude must first be given to Eva Samuel, whose generosity was boundless, and to publisher Charles Miers for suggesting such a worthy subject. Many thanks to Jacques Grange for his support of this book.

This book would never exist if it weren't for my editor, Philip Reeser, whose patience is only matched by his meticulous and stylish eye. Thank you to Henry Connell for his elegant book design. Nina Embiricos, the head of my research team, made a critical contribution with her thoroughness, tenaciousness, and enthusiasm, as did S. Addie McKeon, whose curiosity uncovered many new discoveries.

I am grateful to the clients, friends, family, and associates of Samuel who kindly shared their memories. Samuel's nephew Fred Lanzenberg and longtime friend Arthur Aeschbacher generously gave invaluable insights. My deepest appreciation also goes to Hervé Aaron, Princess Laure de Beauvau-Craon, Antoine Courtois of Atelier Mériguet-Carrère, Alain Demachy, Sylvain Dubuisson, Harold Eberhard Jr., Maria Embiricos, Guillaume Feau, Valentino Garavani, Hubert de Givenchy, Susan Gutfreund, Rodolphe Lasser, David Linker, John Loring, Christian Magot-Cuvrû, Gilles Muller, Countess Isabelle d'Ornano, A. Jerrold Perenchio, Nancy Richardson, Jean-Marie Rossi, Baronne Nadine de Rothschild, Guy de Rougemont, Reggie Sully, and Laurence Tricaud-du Plessix.

Thank you to the following for their essential contributions to our research: James Archer Abbott; Pierre Arizzoli-Clementel; Stephanie Busuttil; Cynthia Cathcart; Jean Emmanuel Chaurrault; Federico Cimatti; Alexandra Cruden; Elizabeth Dunn with the Doris Duke papers at the Duke University Libraries; Christian Duvernois; Peter Edson; Marc Fecker; Feliciano; Brice Foisil; Maureen Footer; Pierre Frey; Melissa Gagen; Jacques Garcia; Yves Gastou; Oberto Gili; Laure de Gramont; Michel Guillard; Terry de Gunzburg; Mick Hales; Francis Hammond; Tanya Hayes; Kelly Konrad; Delphine Krakoff; Rachel Laufer of the Israel Museum, Jerusalem; Sophie Le Tarnec of the Musée Nissim de Camondo; Juan Lluria; Johana Loubet and Tatiana Troubetzkoy at Château Margaux; Brian McCarthy; Rex Miller; Rudolph Netek; David Netto; Christiane de Nicolay-Mazery; Ellen Niven; Mitchell Owens; Béatrice Payet-Godel; Pauline Prévost-Marcilhacy; Jean-Charles de Ravenel; Diana Reeve of Art Resource; Dean Rhys Morgan; Bill Riegel; Sophie Rouart; Henrique Simoes of the Musée des Beaux-Arts, Lyon; and Howard Slatkin.

# NOTES

## I: The Art of the Ensemblier

**1** Often referred to as "Alavoine" during Samuel's time there from about 1946 to 1970, the firm was founded as L. Alavoine et Cie in France in 1887 and L. Alavoine and Co. in the United States in 1893. No records for the firm exist, but it seems sometime after Lucien Alavoine's death in 1917, and almost certainly by the time Samuel worked there, the company dropped the "L" from its name.

**2** The term to describe the interior design professional has constantly changed over time. During most of Samuel's career "interior decorator" was the norm, and this is how he referred to himself.

**3** As explained by Rodolphe Pierre Lasser, who worked for Samuel between 1955 and 1960, in *Le Temps* (Geneva) *Architecture & Design* supplemental magazine, May 3, 2014, p. 8.

**4** Antoinette Berveiller and Gérard Bonal, eds., *Jansen Décoration*, 1971, p. 18.

**5** James Archer Abbott, *Jansen*, 2006, p. 16.

**6** Before Boudin, the firm was criticized for placing more emphasis on elaborate ornament than quality in its Louis Louis–styled rooms. *La Revue de Paris*, January-February 1934, p. 460.

**7** When Jean-Henri died in 1928, his partners were listed as Boudin, along with Gaston Schwartz and Vandries in *Le Figaro*, September 23, 1928, p. 2.

**8** Both firms did work in the contemporary Art Deco style, but at this time, they were more in demand for their historicist work. See Abbott's discussion of this in Abbott, 2006. Alavoine mainly pursued a contemporary idiom for their commercial work, although an Art Deco library created by Martin Becker of the New York office for Mr. and Mrs. Milton Weil, circa 1930, can be viewed at the Brooklyn Museum of Art, Brooklyn, New York.

**9** Jean-Louis Gaillemin, "Henri Samuel: Le conciliateur de l'art modern et de la tradition," *Beaux Arts Magazine*, September 1985, p. 24.

**10** Abbott, *Jansen*, p. 15.

**11** Martin Filler, "Master of the House, Henri Samuel Is the First and Last Word on French Style at Its Grandest," *House & Garden*, July 1989, p. 42.

**12** Abbott, *Jansen*, p. 24.

**13** Ibid, p. 21.

**14** Author telephone interview with James Archer Abbott, June 23, 2017. According to Abbott's research, Boudin, who was married and also had mistresses, frowned upon any hint of homosexuality in the office.

**15** Abbott, *Jansen*, p. 9.

**16** Author interview with Samuel client Nancy Richardson, Shelter Island, New York, August 10, 2017.

**17** Gerry Dryansky, "Henri Samuel Lends a Regal Touch to the Very Rich," *Avenue*, April 1985, p. 176. In various articles, the Vanderbilt family is listed as a particular client of Samuel's. In this interview, Samuel vaguely says he oversaw "the Vanderbilt apartment in New York" while working at Jansen. In other instances, he may also have been alluding to the historic body of work Alavoine (and, by association, Allard) completed for several members of the family.

**18** Nina Embiricos telephone interview with Rodolphe Pierre Lasser, June 30, 2017.

**19** Alavoine rented the avenue Klèber house from the estate of Adolphe Fraenkel, from at least 1935.

**20** James T. Maher, *The Twilight of Splendor: Chronicles of the Age of American Palaces*, New York, 1975. Maher interviewed Samuel in the mid-1960s while researching this account of American palace building.

**21** L. Alavoine et Cie was formed at 9, rue Caumartin, with capital of 500,000 francs in 1887, according to the August 12, 1887, edition of the Paris newspaper *Le Radical*.

**22** *Tapissier-ébéniste* translates to "master furniture maker–upholsterer," but was contemporary parlance for "interior decorator."

**23** Roudillon bought out Emmanuel Ringuet-Leprince in 1885, at the same address, and at an earlier date bought out Gustave Gilbert, whose business dated back to 1830s.

**24** Maher, *The Twilight of Splendor,* 1975.

**25** Mamelsdorf, born in Mannheim, Germany, in 1850, and naturalized as a United States citizen in 1872, divided his time between New York and Paris. His wife Lucie's sister married Nathan Straus Jr., a member of the family who founded the department store R. H. Macy. Several Straus family members commissioned Alavoine to decorate their houses, notably Herbert Straus who purchased several boiseries from Alavoine that were later donated to the Metropolitan Museum of Art and are now part of the Wrightsman Galleries.

**26** John Harris, *Moving Rooms: The Trade in Architectural Salvage*, New Haven, 2007. This book and Bruno Pons's masterful *French Period Rooms 1650–1800*, Dijon, France, 1995, discuss the influence on taste that architectural salvage had in the nineteenth and twentieth centuries.

**27** Maher, *The Twilight of Splendor*, p. 366.

**28** According to Paul Miller, curator at the Preservation Society of Newport County, once Allard merged into Alavoine, Jules Allard's son Fernand, who had been responsible for the Allard New York branch office, became associated with Alavoine and continued to cultivate the same client base while expanding Alavoine's previous scope of operations. S. Addie McKeon telephone and email interview with Paul Miller, May 2017.

**29** At this time, Édouard Fermon became the head of Alavoine New York. Fermon (né Feuermann) was a German who had studied in Paris prior to arriving in New York as an upholsterer for the Herter Brothers. Fluent in English and French and with considerable decorating experience, he established the Alavoine office at 712 Fifth Avenue. Here the firm employed carvers, modelers, plasterers, and painters together with a furniture, curtain, and upholstery departments, with, during its post–First World War heyday, about twenty-five designers. On the death of Fermon in 1932, a corporation was formed headed by Alavoine New York employees Edward Hitau and Martin Becker (d. 1974), formerly of William Baumgarten, New York. The other partner, Édouard Mamelsdorf, died in Paris in 1942. In the teens, Armand-Albert Rateau was the principal designer of the Paris office, until he left for military service during the First World War.

**30** Anna Thomson Dodge, the widow of Horace Elgin Dodge, was married to Hugh Dillman when Rose Terrace II was built. After they divorced in 1947, she returned to using Dodge as her surname.

**31** George Widener would never see the house, perishing with his son in 1912 in the sinking of the *Titanic*. His widow, Eleanor, survived on a lifeboat and supervised the completion of Miramar, where she lived with her second husband, Alexander Rice.

**32** Delphine Dodge married three times before her death in 1943: to James Cromwell (1920–1928); Raymond Baker (1928–1935); and Timothy Godde (1935–1943). Upon her marriage to Godde, she left the Washington D.C. house to live in Rye, New York. Around this time, Anna Thomson Dodge allowed Delphine's former mother-in-law Eva Stotesbury, who had suffered financial reverses, to live in the Washington house.

**33** Henri Martin (d. 1968), a nephew of Lucien Alavoine, took control of Alavoine in Paris after Lucien's death in 1917. On the death of Édouard Hitau, who ran the New York office, Martin Becker became associated with Jean-Georges Rueff, in the management of the New York branch which Becker closed in 1964. Alavoine-Paris, located at 42, avenue Kleber, closed in 1970, according Miller interview, May 2017.

**34** Jansen continued to operate, with Paul Manno overseeing the New York operations and Pierre Delbée, Paris. For a discussion of Jansen's later history, see Abbott, *Jansen*, pp. 35–40.

**35** Pierre Delbée, "Propos sur le métier de décorateur," *Les Antiquaires et Les Decorateurs* exhibition catalogue, Paris, 1962, p. 42.

## II: Restoration

1 S. J. Perelman, "Westward Ha!," *The Most of S. J. Perelman*, New York, 1958, p. 386.

2 These efforts increased under André Malraux's tenure as cultural minister from 1959 to 1976. He initiated programs to clean Paris's building façades, restore the palace of Versailles, and more.

3 Carlhian were specialists in boiseries and Alavoine's neighbor on the avenue Kléber. Before the Second World War, they worked extensively with Duveen to furnish the new American palaces and considered Alavoine's New York office its greatest competition.

4 Ian Skye, "French Period Decoration in the Mode of Henri Samuel of Alavoine," *Apollo*, December 1955, p. 208.

5 Ibid.

6 Nina Embiricos interview with Arthur Aeschbacher, artist and longtime friend of Samuel, May 4, 2017.

7 Gloria Braggiotti Etting, "Phila. Notables Enjoy Gay Reunion in Paris," *The Philadelphia Inquirer*, July 10, 1949, p. B1.

8 Gary Cohen, "The Legend of Rubirosa," *Vanity Fair*, November 2002.

9 "Le style 'Maison de Campagne Familiale,'" *Connaissance des Arts*, August 1952, p. 44.

10 As quoted in Jean Bothorel, *Louise, ou, La vie de Louise de Vilmorin*, Paris, 1995, p. 174.

11 "La Rentrée", *Maison et Jardin*, October-November 1953, p. 50.

12 "M. Henri Samuel, Decorateur: Les secrets de l'elegance," *Connaissance des Arts*, December 1959, pp. 140–49.

13 The staircase was copied after one from a Rothschild house. Just like the paneling that would be donated to the Museum of Israel, the staircase came from the Louis XV Parisian house of Jacques-Samuel Bernard. Baron Edmond de Rothschild (the grandfather of Samuel's client of the same name) acquired these architectural elements and incorporated them into the Hôtel de Pontalba in the mid-nineteenth century.

14 Paul Guth, "La Douceur de ton du dix-huitième siècle cadre très bien avec les tableaux plus hardis de couleurs," *Connaissance des Arts*, August 1958, pp. 22–25.

15 Embiricos interview with Aeschbacher.

16 Queiroz Pereira in correspondence dated November 24, 1959, as cited by http://press.fourseasons.com/lisbon/trending-now/hotel-history/

17 Helder Carita, Ritz: *Forty Years in Lisbon*, Lisbon, 2000.

18 "M. Henri Samuel, Decorateur: Les Secrets de L'élégance." *Connaissance des Arts*, December 1959, pp. 140–49.

19 Jean-Louis Gaillemin, "*Henri Samuel: l'art d'installer des collections*," *Beaux Arts Magazine*, September 1985, p. 26.

20 The Mobilier National is the French agency responsible for the conservation of state furniture. It traces its origins back to Louis XIV and the royal Gobelins and Beauvais workshops.

21 Denise Ledoux-Lebard, *Le Grand Trianon: Meubles et objets d'art, tome I*, Paris, 1975.

22 "Au château de Versailles: Un Appartement où l'on vit," *Maison et Jardin*, May 1967.

## III: Le Goût Rothschild

1 Guy de Rothschild, *The Whims of Fortune: The Memoirs of Guy de Rothschild*, New York, 1985, p. 6.

2 Nadine de Rothschild, *La Baronne rentre à cinq heures*, Paris, 1987, p. 140.

3 Arnault-Plessis, "Château de fêtes du temps des crinolines: Férrieres," *Plaisir de France*, December 1969, p. 68.

4 For a history of the Rothschilds' collecting, see Pauline Prévost-Marcilhacy, *Les Rothschild: Batisseurs et mécènes*, Paris, 1995.

5 Bruno Pons, *French Period Rooms 1650–1800*. Dijon France, 1995, pp. 61–64.

6 Niall Ferguson, *The House of Rothschild: Money's Prophets*, 1798–1848, vol. 1, 1999, pp. 481–85.

7 John Harris, *Moving Rooms: The Trade in Architectural Salvage*, New Haven, 2007, p. 65.

8 Pauline Prévost-Marcilhacy, ed., *Les Rothschild: Une dynastie de mécènes en France*, Paris, 2016, p. 338

9 The duc d'Aumale was the son of France's last monarch, Louis Philippe. He was forced into exile from 1848 to 1871, after the abolishment of the monarchy.

10 See Prévost-Marcilhacy, ed., *Les Rothschild*, vol. 1, pp. 118–33.

11 See "Once Upon a Time" for the Baron's full remembrance of Ferriéres, G. de Rothschild, *Whims of Fortune*, pp. 5–28.

12 These hangings would later be installed in the Baron and Baronne Guy's residence in the Hôtel Lambert on the Île Saint-Louis, Paris.

13 Christopher Petkanas, "Staying Power," *Women's Wear Daily*, June 29, 1986.

14 Charlotte Aillaud, "Design Dialogue: Henri Samuel, the Eminence Grise of French Design," *Architectural Digest*, July 1989, p. 60.

15 Pierre Descargues, "Leçon d'art dans un parc (En Normandie chez la baronne Alex de Rothschild)," *Plaisir de France*, June 1972, pp. 32–37.

16 When the marriage dissolved in 1956, Alix de Rothschild lived at the Château de Reux and the couple's avenue Foch residence.

17 Petkanas, "Staying Power."

18 Edmond de Rothschild, "Hommage à Henri Samuel" in Christie's *Succession de M. Henri Samuel*. Monte Carlo, Monaco, December 15, 1996, p. 10

19 This was facilitated by the Rothschild family's system of marking their storage crates in their signature colors as well as by sophisticated inventories.

20 Élie de Rothschild in Françoise Cachin, ed., *Pillages et restitutions: Le destin des œuvres d'art sorties de France pendant la Seconde Guerre mondiale*. Paris, 1997, p. 61.

21 Christiane de Nicolay-Mazery and Jean-Bernard Naudin, *The French Chateau: Life, Style, Tradition*, London, 1991, p. 184.

22 Stated in a video interview made by the New York antique dealers Rosenberg and Stiebel.

23 Edmond de Rothschild, in *Succession de M. Henri Samuel*, 1996, p. 10.

24 N. de Rothschild, *La Baronne*, pp. 128–29.

25 Ibid.

26 The author is unable to determine if this was an actual lodge or an imagined one.

27 Nina Embiricos correspondence with Baronne Nadine de Rothschild, August 12, 2017.

28 Ibid.

29 During the Second World War, this *hôtel* was used as the Luftwaffe officers' club. It was later sold to the United States for its ambassador's residence.

30 Karl Katz, *The Exhibitionist: Living Museums, Loving Museums*, New York, 2016.

31 Jean-Louis Gaillemin, "Henri Samuel: L'art d'installer des collections," *Beaux Arts Magazine*, September 1985, p. 27.

32 Gerry Dryansky, "Henri Samuel Lends a Regal Touch to the Very Rich," *Avenue*, April 1985, p. 176.

## IV: The Mix Master

1 Charlotte Aillaud, "Design Dialogue: Henri Samuel, the Eminence Grise of French Design," *Architectural Digest*, January 1989, p. 60.

2 Jean-Louis Gaillemin, "Henri Samuel: L'art d'installer des collections," *Beaux Arts Magazine*, September 1985, p. 26.

3 Jean Clair, "The Lure of Chassy: A Legacy of Balthus in the Morvan Hills of France," *Architectural Digest*, December 1984, pp. 186–87.

4 Author interview with Eva Samuel, Paris, May 2016.

5 Balthus and Alain Vircondelet, *Vanished Splendors: A Memoir*, New York, 2002, pp. 141–42.

6 Author interview with Samuel client Susan Gutfreund, New York, March 18, 2015.

7 Nina Embiricos telephone interview with Arthur Aeschbacher, May 2017.

8 Ibid.

9 Yvonne Brunhammer, "Le 'Decor' Samuel," *Connaissance des Arts*, December 1996.

10 Samuel first worked with George Embiricos in the 1950s on his apartment at 740 Park Avenue in New York.

11 Daniel Marchesseau, *Diego Giacometti*, Paris, 1987, p. 65.

12 Samuel most likely purchased the entire edition of six from Rougemont, keeping some for himself and placing others with clients over time. This Nuage table and two additional ones featuring chromed steel tops were included in the 1996 Christie's sale of Samuel's estate.

13 Anne-Marie Fève, "Atelier A, L'argot de l'art," *Libération*, October 1, 2003.

14 Pierre Restany, "Manifeste de l'Atelier A," January 1970.

15 Nina Embiricos correspondence with Baronne Nadine de Rothschild, August 26, 2017.

16 Brunhammer, "Le 'Decor' Samuel." Henri most likely first discovered the artist at the Heller Gallery in New York in 1987.

**17** Author correspondence with Sylvain Dubuisson, August 12, 2017.

**V: Henri Samuel Décorateur**

**1** "Henri Samuel Décorateur" was the official name Samuel used when registering with the French government.

**2** Samuel worked with the Shah of Iran and several members of his family from the late 1960s until 1979, when the shah was overthrown. David Linker remembers sharing his workspace with enormous curtains that were destined for a palace in Tehran. The Aga Khan IV also commissioned Samuel to decorate his *château* outside Chantilly, the epicenter of French horse racing. Apparently the Aga Khan, who was such a voracious collector of pictures, ran out of wall space, forcing Samuel to hang additional ones atop existing framed mirrors.

**3** Nina Embiricos telephone interview with Christian Magot-Cuvrû, July 19, 2017.

**4** Author interview with David Linker, New York, March 7, 2017.

**5** Nina Embiricos telephone interview with Antoine Courtois, July 27, 2017.

**6** Nina Embiricos telephone interview with Samuel's nephew Fred Lanzenberg, August 22, 2017.

**7** The French second floor is termed "third floor" in American English.

**8** This was not always the case. So uncomfortable were Élie and Liliane de Rothschild at the Hôtel de Masseran that they had to explicitly ask Victor Grandpierre to supply them with chairs they could relax in.

**9** Georgina Oliver, "Polonaise with Love: The Most Romantic Apartment in Paris," *Vogue*, May 1976, p. 195.

**10** Christiane de Nicolay-Mazery, *Private Houses of Paris*, New York, 2000.

**11** Ibid.

**12** Michel d'Ornano, Hubert's brother, was also a longtime client of Samuel.

**13** Nicholas Faith, *Chateau Margaux*, Paris, 2005, p. 14.

**14** Jean-Louis Gaillemin, "Un 'château' du Médoc à la simplicité confortable," *Le Figaro Magazine*, November 12, 1983, p. 212.

**15** Steven A. L. Aronson, "The Vintage Life of Château Margaux," *House & Garden*, August 1984, p. 146.

**16** Ibid.

**17** Ibid.

**18** Embiricos interview with Magot-Cuvrû.

**19** Leslie George, "In Paris: At the Home of the Count de Camondo," *M: The Civilized Man*, February 1987, p. 38.

**20** The "Pour Camondo" committee meeting records conserved at the Musée Nissim de Camondo were consulted in the preparation of this chapter.

**21** Dana Thomas, "Imperial Splendor," *Architectural Digest*, October 2012.

**22** Jean Bond Rafferty, "Gentleman Decorator," *Town & Country*, November 1995.

**VI: F.F.F.**

**1** Bernard Berenson, entry for May 26, 1956, in Nicky Mariano and Iris Origo, *Sunset and Twilight*, 1963, p. 547.

**2** This is from Eugenia Sheppard's syndicated column that Billy Baldwin guest wrote. "Travel A to S in Design and Decor," *Minneapolis Star*, August 24, 1962: 6B. For the "F" entry, Baldwin writes "FASH-ION—to be avoided if it prevents personal taste and creates uniformity. Old families in the South were classified as F.F.V. (First Families of Virginia); now there is a class of Americans under the heading of F.F.F. (Fine French Furniture), many of whom have adopted this taste out of pure snobbery."

**3** Eleanor Page, "Benefit Opening of Restaurant Is El-egant," *Chicago Tribune*, December 10, 1963. The dinner concluded with the show "Debut de Maxim," which featured the actor Jean-Pierre Aumont and a Christian Dior fashion show, with head designer Marc Bohan in attendance.

**4** "Mrs. Byron C. Foy, A Society Leader," *New York Times*, August, 21, 1957, p. 27.

**5** Khoi Nguyen, "Gilt Complex," *Connoisseur*, September 1991.

**6** Rosamond Bernier, "Palm Beach Fable: The Private Wrightsman Rooms," *House & Garden*, May 1984. Boudin supplied parquetry de Versailles from Cardinal Richelieu's rooms at the Palais Royal.

**7** Peter Wilson, then chairman of the auction house Sotheby's that was auctioning off the house's contents at this time, quoted in Bernier, May 1984, pp. 118–35.

**8** Nguyen, "Gilt Complex," p. 117.

**9** Ibid, p. 77.

**10** Bernier, "Palm Beach Fable," p. 222.

**11** Author correspondence with James Archer Abbott, July 4, 2017.

**12** Bernier, "Palm Beach Fable," p. 222. In the 1970s the Wrightsmans bought ivory furniture made in India for colonial governors—from Mentmore, the Rothschild-Rosebery house in Buckinghamshire—or their salmon-pink reception room. "Lady Rose-bery never liked them, so she let us buy them."

**13** Bruno Pons, *French Period Room 1650–1800*, Dijon, France, 1995.

**14** Jean-Louis Gaillemin, "Henri Samuel: L'art d'installer des collections," *Beaux Arts Magazine*, September 1985, p. 27.

**15** Danielle Kisluk-Gorsheide and Jeffrey Munger, *The Wrightsman Galleries for French Decorative Arts*, New Haven, 2010, p. 12.

**16** Rita Reif, "It's Almost Like Being at a Palace in France," *New York Times*, December 10, 1973, p. 49.

**17** Author interview with lighting specialist William Riegler, who worked at the Metropolitan Museum of Art during the Linsky installation.

**18** Reif, "It's Almost Like Being at a Palace in France," p. 49.

**19** The boiseries are thought to have passed through Jansen's hands in the 1930s.

**20** James Parker, "The French Eighteenth-Century Room in the Newly Re-opened Wrightsman Galleries," *Apollo*, December 1977, p. 384.

**21** Ibid.

**22** In 2006 this room was reinterpreted as a bed chamber.

**23** Samuel also worked with Arthur Rosenblatt, the museum's vice president for architecture and planning, and architect Robert Kupiec. Stanley Abercrombie, "Museum Caliber," *Interior Design*, July 1985.

**24** Christopher Buckley, "A Passion for French Style: Lee Thaw's Old World Maisonette in Manhattan," *Architectural Digest*, October 1986, p. 224.

**25** *Washington Post* syndicated column, "French Throw 'Dazzling' Party," *Tampa Bay Times* (St. Petersburg, Florida), May 20, 1976, p. 2A.

**26** Author interview with Nancy Richardson, Shelter Island, New York, August 10, 2017.

**27** Ibid.

**28** "Eye Scoop?," *Women's Wear Daily*, October 16, 1987, p. 6.

**29** Jamee Gregory, *New York Apartments: Private Views*, New York, 2008.

**30** Ibid.

**31** Author interview with Susan Gutfreund, New York, March 2015.

**32** Atelier Mériguet-Carrère was Samuel's preferred painters. See chapter five for more about his work with the firm.

**33** A. Jerrold Perenchio and Margie Perenchio, *875 Nimes: The House and Gardens*, privately printed, 1995, p. 17.

**34** Ibid.

**35** Ibid, pp. 28–29.

**36** Ibid.

**VII: Legacy**

**1** Nina Embiricos correspondence with Hubert de Givenchy, September 12, 2017.

**2** Several pieces that Samuel commissioned from Philippe Hiquily and Guy de Rougemont are con-sidered by the artists as "Henry Samuel editions," because Samuel gave input on the design.

**3** Nina Embiricos telephone interview with Yves Gastou, May 3, 2017.

**4** Jennifer Krichels, "The Enduring Legacy of Henri Samuel, Decorator to the Wealthy," *Financial Times*, November 21, 2014.

**5** Nina Embiricos telephone interview with Rodolphe Pierre Lasser, June 30, 2017.

**6** Jean Bond Rafferty, "Jacques Grange," *Town & Country*, January 2001.

**7** Jean Bond Rafferty, "Poetic License," *Architectural Digest*, May 2011, pp. 154–61.

**8** James Reginato, "Monuments Man," *Vanity Fair*, January 2016.

**9** Nina Embiricos telephone interview with Christian Magot-Cuvrû, July 19, 2017.

**10** James Reginato, "The Grand Style of Jacques Garcia," *Sotheby's at Auction*, November 2012.

**11** Nina Embiricos correspondence with Delphine Krakoff, August 23, 2017.

**12** Author telephone interview with Brian J. McCarthy, June 30, 1017.

# BIBLIOGRAPHY

Abbott, James Archer. *Jansen*. New York: Acanthus Press, 2006.

Abercrombie, Stanley. "Museum Caliber." *Interior Design* (July 1985): 212–21.

Aillaud, Charlotte. "Design Dialogue: Henri Samuel, the Eminence Grise of French Design." *Architectural Digest* (January 1989): 50, 54, 60, 68.

———. "Architectural Digest Visits: Diego Giacometti." *Architectural Digest* (September 1990): 94–99.

Arnault-Plessis. "Château de fêtes du temps des crinolines: Ferrières." *Plaisir de France* (December 1969): 66–73.

Aronson, Steven A. L. "The Vintage Life of Château Margaux." *House & Garden* (August 1984): 134–46.

Assouline, Pierre. *Le dernier des Camondo*. Paris: Éditions Gallimard, 2010.

"Au château de Versailles: Un Appartement où l'on vit." *Maison et Jardin* (May 1967).

Balthus and Alain Vircondelet. *Vanished Splendors: A Memoir*. New York: HarperCollins, 2002.

Benhamou-Huet, Judith. "Dans l'hôtel particulier de Robert de Balkany." *Les Echos* (September 16, 2016): 39.

Bernier, Rosamond. "Palm Beach Fable: The Private Wrightsman Rooms." *House & Garden* (May 1984): 118–35.

Berr de Turique, Marcelle. "Un Salon 18e à Jerusalem." *Connaissance des Arts* (October 1969): 130–35.

Berveiller, Antoinette, and Gérard Bonal, eds. *Jansen Décoration*. Paris: Société d'Etudes et de Publications Economiques, 1971.

Boodro, Michael. "The Rothschild Style." *Vogue* (November 1988), 404–13.

Bothorel, Jean. *Louise, ou, La vie de Louise de Vilmorin*. Paris: Grasset, 1995.

Bourdet, Denise. "Château Lafite Rothschild 1961." *Connaissance des Arts* (August 1961): 46–55.

Brunhammer, Yvonne. "Le 'Décor' Samuel." *Connaissance des Arts* (December 1996): 98–105.

Buckley, Christopher. "A Passion for French Style: Lee Thaw's Old World Maisonette in Manhattan." *Architectural Digest* (October 1986): 152–57.

Cachin, Françoise. *Pillages et restitutions: le destin des œuvres d'art sorties de France pendant la Seconde Guerre mondiale*. Paris: Direction des musées de France, 1997.

Capitani, Jean-Paul, ed. *Le Choix de la modernité: Rodin, Lam, Picasso, Bacon: Jacqueline Delubac*. Lyon: Musée des Beaux-Arts, 2014.

Carita, Helder. *Ritz: Forty Years in Lisbon*. Lisbon: Hotel Ritz SA, 2000.

"Centenaire d'une Grande Demeure." *Maison et Jardin* (December 1959): 70–78.

Christie's. *Appartement Parisien de M. et Mme John Gutfreund*. Paris: Christie's, June 28, 2012.

———. *Succesion de M. Henri Samuel*. Monte Carlo, Monaco: Christie's, December 15, 1996.

Clair, Jean. "The Lure of Chassy: A Legacy of Balthus in the Morvan Hills of France." *Architectural Digest* (December 1984): 186–94.

Clarke, Gerald. "Henri Samuel." *Architectural Digest* (January 2010): 97.

Coche de La Ferté, Étienne. "Le Faubourg Saint-Germain dans l'Orient séditieux." *L'Oeil* (August–September 1969): 20–27.

Cooper, Douglas. *Les Grandes Collections Privées*. Paris: Pont Royal, 1963.

Craven, Wayne. *Gilded Mansions: Grand Architecture and High Society*. New York: W. W. Norton & Company, 2008.

Dampierre, Florence de. *The Decorator*. New York: Rizzoli, 1989.

Delbée, Pierre. "Propos sur le métier de décorateur." *Les Antiquaires et Les Decorateurs*, exhibition catalogue. Paris: Syndicat National des Antiquaires, 1962: 43–46.

Demoriane, Hélène. "Le Plus Spectaculaire des châteaux batis en France au XIX siècle: Ferrières." *Connaissance des Arts* (July 1963): 74–87.

Dumesnil, Jeannie. "Tapis d'aujourd'hui, tapis de demain." *L'Oeil* (October 1962): 74–84.

Faith, Nicholas. *Château Margaux*. Paris: Flammarion, 2005.

Favardin, Patrick, and Guy Bloch-Champfort. *Decorators of the 60s and 70s*. Paris: Éditions Norma, 2015.

Ferrand, Franck. *Gérald Van der Kemp: Un gentilhomme à Versailles*. Paris: Perrin, 2005.

Filler, Martin. "Master of the House, Henri Samuel Is the First and Last Word on French Style at Its Grandest." *House & Garden* (July 1989): 42.

Fregnac, Claude. "Henri Samuel: Le conciliateur de l'art moderne et de la tradition." *Réalités* (November 1976): 60–67.

Fregnac, Claude, and Wayne Andrews. *The Great Houses of Paris*. New York: Viking Press, 1979.

Gaigneron, Axelle de. "Un décorateur Français au Met." *Connaissance des Arts* (November 1984): 96–99.

Gaillemin, Jean-Louis. "Henri Samuel: l'art d'installer des collections." *Beaux Arts Magazine* (September 1985): 26–27.

———."Un 'château' du Médoc à la simplicité confortable." *Le Figaro Magazine* (November 12, 1983): 212–16.

Galerie du Passage. *Rougemont: Ellipse et cylindre, volumes polychromes 1965–1975*. Paris: Galerie du Passage, 2003.

Garavani, Valentino, and André Leon Talley. *Valentino: At the Emperor's Table*. New York: Assouline, 2014.

Greene, Elaine. "The Man with the French Polish: Restorer D. Linker," *House & Garden* (April 1986): 66.

Gregory, Jamee. *New York Apartments: Private Views*. New York: Rizzoli, 2004.

Guth, Paul. "La Douceur de ton du dix-huitième siècle cadre très bien avec les tableaux plus hardis de couleurs." *Connaissance des Arts* (August 1958): 22–25.

Harris, John. *Moving Rooms: The Trade in Architectural Salvage*. New Haven: Yale University Press, 2007.

"Hommage à Henri Samuel." *Connaissance des Arts* (February 1997): 113.

Humphries, Oscar. "The Attitude of Artistry." *Apollo* (March 2011): 114–19.

"In Chicago, It's Maxim's: Interiors by H. Samuel and Others." *Interiors* (November 1964): 68–69.

Irving, Carolina, Miguel Flores-Vianna, and Charlotte di Carcaci. "Babylon Revisited." *New York Times* (October 20, 2013): SMA70.

Katz, Karl. *The Exhibitionist: Living Museums, Loving Museums*. New York: Overlook Press, 2016.

Kernan, Thomas, ed. *Les Réussites de la Décoration Française 1950–1960*. Paris: Éditions du Pont Royal, 1960.

———. *The Finest Rooms in France*. New York: Viking Press, 1967.

Kingdom of Belgium Federal Public Service, ed. *Belgian Embassy Washington.* Brussels: Dirk Achten, 2010.

Kisluk-Gorsheide, Danielle, and Jeffrey Munger. *The Wrightsman Galleries for French Decorative Arts.* New Haven: Yale University Press, 2010.

Krichels, Jennifer. "The Enduring Legacy of Henri Samuel, Decorator to the Wealthy," *Financial Times* (November 21, 2014).

"La Rentrée." *Maison et Jardin* (October–November 1953): 50–51.

"La vie d'été: en Normandie, au Cottage de Reux." *Maison et Jardin* (June–July 1958): 78–81.

"Le Château de Reux: Perle du pays d'auge." *Maison et Jardin* (September–October 1957): 56–61.

"Le Style 'Maison de Campagne Familiale.'" *Connaissance des Arts* (August 1952): 44–47.

Ledoux-Lebard, Denise. *Le Grand Trianon: Meubles et objets d'art, tome I.* Paris: Éditions des Musées Nationaux, 1975.

Leymarie, Jean. "Balthus at the Villa Medici." *House & Garden* (January 1984): 54–63.

"M. Henri Samuel, Decorator: Les Secrets de l'elegance." *Connaissance des Arts* (December 1959): 140–49.

Maher, James T. *The Twilight of Splendor: Chronicles of the Age of American Palaces.* New York: Little Brown & Co., 1975.

Mansfield, Stephanie. *The Richest Girl in the World: The Extravagant Life and Fast Times of Doris Duke.* New York: G.P. Putnam and Sons, 1992.

Marchesseau, Daniel. *Diego Giacometti.* Paris: Hermann, 1987.

Matzig, Katharina. "The Ritz in Lisbon." *Baumeister* (February 2004): 18–19.

McCall, Patricia. "Parisian Splendor: Home Design." *New York Times* (February 12, 1984).

Medford, Sarah. "The Ultimate Francophile." *Town & Country* (April 2010): 77.

Meenan, Monica. "French Influence." *Town & Country* (April 1982): 201–.

Menkes, Suzy. "Henri Samuel, the Gentleman-Decorator." *International Herald Tribune,* Paris (November 26, 1996): 11.

Messelet, Jean. *Musée Nissim de Camondo.* Paris: Union Centrale des arts décoratifs, 1966.

Mouillefarine, Laurence. "Henri Samuel: France's Supreme Master of Progressive Historicism." *Architectural Digest* (January 2000): 224.

Nanteuil, Luc de. "Un Grand Mécène, Jayne Wrightsman." *Connaissance des Arts* (December 1992): 32–41.

Nguyen, Khoi. "Gilt Complex." *Connoisseur* (September 1991): 75–77, 116–17.

Nicolay-Mazery, Christine de. *Private Houses of France: Living with History.* Paris: Flammarion, 2014.

———. *Private Houses of Paris.* New York: Vendome: 2000.

Nicolay-Mazery, Christiane de, and Jean-Bernard Naudin. *The French Chateau: Life, Style, Tradition.* London: Thames and Hudson, 1991.

Oliver, Georgina. "Polonaise with Love: The Most Romantic Apartment in Paris." *Vogue* (May 1976): 194–97, 214.

Owens, Mitchell. "Samuel at Ninety." *Nest* (Fall 1999): 58–73.

Panafieu, Anne de. "L'appartement d'Henri Samuel: Une Synthese de l'ancien et du la moderne." *L'Oeil* (September 1978): 52–57.

Parker, James. "The Hôtel de Varengeville Room and the Room from the Palais Paar: A Magnificent Donation." *Metropolitan Museum of Art Bulletin* (November 1969).

Peck, Amelia, James Parker, William Rieder, Olga Raggio, Mary B. Shepard, Annie-Christine Daskalakis Mathews, Daniélle O. Kisluk-Grosheide, Wolfram Koeppe, Joan R. Mertens, Alfreda Murck, and Wen C. Fong. *Period Rooms in the Metropolitan Museum of Art.* New York: Metropolitan Museum of Art, 1996.

Perenchio, A. Jerrold and Margie. *875 Nîmes: The House and Gardens.* Self-published, Bel Air, California: 1995.

Petkanas, Christopher. "Chichi Devil." *The New York Times Magazine* (February 22, 2009): 132.

———. "Interior Design Loses Regal Touch with Henri Samuel's Retirement." *Women's Wear Daily* (June 29, 1986).

Pons, Bruno. *French Period Rooms 1650–1800.* Dijon France: Éditions Faton, 1995.

Prévost-Marcilhacy, Pauline. *Les Rothschild: Batisseurs et mécènes.* Paris: Flammarion, 1995.

Prévost-Marcilhacy, Pauline, ed. *Les Rothschild: une dynastie de mécènes en France.* Paris: Co-published by Musée du Louvre, BnF and Somogy, 2016.

Rafferty, Jean Bond. "A Haven in Paris." *Town & Country* (October 2003): 178–86, 216.

———. "French Expressionism." *Town & Country* (November 1996): 152.

———. "Gentleman Decorator." *Town & Country* (November 1995): 150–57, 204.

———. "Jacques Grange." *Town & Country* (January 2001).

———. "Parisian Panache: With a French Master as Her Mentor, an American Creates a Home on the Left Bank." *Veranda* (January–February 2010): 74–.

Reginato, James. "The Book of Samuel." *House & Garden* (January 1997): 112–17.

Reif, Rita. "A Birthday Cake of a Room." *New York Times* (November 22, 1969): 42.

Rense, Paige, ed. *Architectural Digest: International Interiors.* Los Angeles: Knapp Press, 1979.

Rewald, Sabine. *Balthus: Cats and Girls.* New York: Metropolitan Museum of Art, 2013.

Richardson, Nancy. "A Talent for Houses: Interior Designer Henri Samuel's House in Paris Reveals his Instinct for Beauty." *House & Garden* (March 1984): 154–60.

Rothschild, Guy de. *The Whims of Fortune: The Memoirs of Guy de Rothschild.* New York: Random House, 1985.

Rothschild, Nadine de. *La Baronne rentre à cinq heures.* Paris: Éditions de la Seine, 1987.

Samuel, Henri. "Alavoine a signé cette installation." *France Illustration: Le Monde Illustré* (April 15, 1950): n.p.

Scott, Barbara. "The Rothschild Room in the Louvre." *Apollo* (October 1991): 270–71.

Shaw, Mark, photographer. "High Style at Low Cost." *Life* (March 14, 1960): 50–54.

Skye, Ian. "French Period Decoration in the Mode of Henri Samuel of Alavoine." *Apollo* (December 1955): 208–09.

Sotheby Parke Bernet. *Property from the Collection of Mrs. Charles Wrightsman Removed from her Palm Beach Residence.* New York: Sotheby's, May 5, 1984.

Sotheby's. *Meubles et Objets d'Art provenant du Chateau de Ferrières appartenant au Baron Guy de Rothschild.* Monaco: Sotheby's, December 3, 1994.

———. *Property from the Collection of Mrs. Charles Wrightsman: The London Residence.* New York: Sotheby's, April 28, 2010.

———. *Robert de Balkany: rue de Varenne,* vols. I and II. Paris: Sotheby's, September 28 and 29, 2016.

Storey, Walter Rendell. "Fine and Decorative Art on Exhibit." *New York Times* (November 4, 1934): X11.

Sverbeyeff, Elizabeth. "In a Paris Mood." *New York Times* (June 27, 1965): SM36.

Taylor, John. "Hard to Be Rich: The Rise and Wobble of the Gutfreunds." *New York* (January 11, 1988): 22–32.

"The Ritz in Lisbon," *Interior Design* (October 1961): 170.

Thomas, Dana. "Imperial Splendor." *Architectural Digest* (October 2012): 128–.

Toll, Roger, and André Leon Talley. "Modern Rothschild." *House & Garden* (March 1980): 125–37.

Van der Kemp, Gérald. *Directoire–Empire–Consulat: Guide Officiel.* Paris: Éditions des Musées Nationaux, 1958.

Van der Kemp, Gérald, and Pierre Lemoine. *Versailles et Trianon.* Versailles: Éditions d'art Lys, 1979.

Vickers, Hugo, ed. *Alexis: The Memoirs of Baron de Redé.* Dorset: Estate of the late Baron de Redé, 2005.

# INDEX

# IMAGE CREDITS

Page 2: The *grand salon* of the Paris apartment of
Countess Isabel d'Ornano in 2000, nearly twenty-five
years after Henri Samuel first decorated it for the
countess and her husband, Count Hubert d'Ornano.

Pages 4–5: Christa Päffgen, better known as Nico,
models a contemporary fashion for *Life* magazine in
Henri Samuel's Paris living room, 1960.

Page 250: A rendering by Jeremiah Goodman of the
*grand salon* at La Bouteriez, Samuel's country house
in Montfort l'Amaury.

First published in the United States of America in 2018 by
Rizzoli International Publications, Inc.
300 Park Avenue South
New York, NY 10010
www.rizzoliusa.com

Copyright © 2018 by Rizzoli International Publications, Inc.
Text: Copyright © 2018 by Emily Evans Eerdmans
ISBN: 978-0-8478-6186-6
Library of Congress Control Number: 2017951934

For Rizzoli International Publications:
Philip Reeser, Editor
Maria Pia Gramaglia, Production Manager
Elizabeth Smith, Copy Editor

Design: Henry Connell
Printed and bound in China
2018 2019 2020 2021 / 10 9 8 7 6 5 4 3 2 1